RAIL CENTRES:
BRIGHTON

RAIL CENTRES:
BRIGHTON

B.K.COOPER

LONDON

IAN ALLAN LTD

Title page: (Left) **Brighton station frontage, with Mocatta's station house and the characteristic clock still visible between the awnings and the two gables of the roof.** *British Rail*

(Right) **Stroudley and R. J. Billinton engines at Brighton mpd near the turn of the century. In the foreground are two Stroudley Class D 0-4-2 tanks, Nos 231,** *Horsham,* **and 28,** *Isfield,* **with Billinton's Class D3 0-4-4T No 398, visible behind them. To the right are Billinton 'E4' 0-6-2T No 493,** *Telscombe,* **and Stroudley 'E' class 0-6-0T No 116,** *Tournai.* **Behind them are Billinton 'E4' No 494,** *Woodgate,* **and Stroudley Class E No 97,** *Honfleur.* *IAL*

Below: **Class C2X 0-6-0 No 32449 crosses the Lewes Road Viaduct with a train of passenger stock to be used in a Civil Defence exercise at Kemp Town station on 28 September 1958.** *W. M. Jackson*

First published 1981

Second impression 1991

ISBN 0 7110 1155 1

Published by Ian Allan Ltd, Shepperton, Surrey, and printed in the United Kingdom by Ian Allan Printing Ltd at their works at Coombelands in Runnymede, England

Contents

Preface

Asked by a BBC interviewer why he came to Brighton, a visitor exclaimed 'It's all that lovely sea!' One can imagine the sweeping gesture accompanying the remark, taking in the whole panorama from Seaford Head in one direction to Worthing Pier in the other, with the gentle hump of Cissbury half-way to the west recalling the proximity of the Downs. No doubt Neolithic Man, pausing from his labours in the Cissbury flint mines, refreshed himself similarly by gazing out to sea. It is a spectacle which mysteriously combines the infinitely changing and the everlasting. Some of this charisma must have rubbed off on the London, Brighton & South Coast Railway. An unusual livery, named locomotives, and a mechanical engineer voted by common consent to be a member of the railway pantheon are not sufficient in themselves to explain the esteem in which it is held. Some weight must be given, however, to the effect of early electrification, so that as long ago as the 1930s, when nostalgia was considered an emotion suitable only for aged nannies, there were many who clung devotedly to their memories of the line before this awful occurrence. Did they create for themselves a Golden Age that never really existed? A lot of us who lived north of the Thames used to suspect it. On the other hand the very fact that main line Brighton steam was so abruptly extinguished casts an insidious spell. 'What song the Syrens sang' will ever excite curiosity but elude an answer. I doubt if one can get much closer to the real London, Brighton & South Coast Railway, but it is always fun to try. There are many routes to follow – old timetables, locomotive history, rolling stock and signalling, and so on. Most of them are well trodden. In this book I have given considerable weight to contemporary comment in newspapers, magazines and other less ephemeral writings, for these, I think, bring us as close to the goal as it is possible to get. They also show us Brighton the town, and Brighton is inseparable from the London, Brighton & South Coast Railway.

I acknowledge with gratitude the help and interest of the staffs at the Public Libraries of Brighton and Hove, the National Railway Museum, and the Press Office of the Southern Region at Waterloo, who furnished the contacts and other facilities without which a book such as this could not be written. I am also much indebted to Mr A. B. MacLeod, who has only to look at an LBSC locomotive number to divine at once its class, wheel arrangement and many a curious genealogical detail, and to my son Martin who has similar gifts covering more recent history. My thanks, also, to Mr R. C. Riley for help, advice, and the first-hand experience of Brighton under fire during World War 2 related in Appendix 2.

Stoneleigh, Surrey
February 1981

6

1. First Trains to Brighton

'But have we any leisure for a description of Brighton? – for Brighton, a clean Naples with genteel Lazaroni; for Brighton, that always looks brisk, gay and gaudy like a harlequin's jacket; for Brighton, which used to be seven hours distant from London at the time of our story, which is now only a hundred minutes off, and which may approach who knows how much nearer . . .'

The Brighton scenes in *Vanity Fair* are set in the year of Waterloo but here Thackeray is apostrophising the Brighton of the 1840s. His novel was published in 1847, by which time the acceleration he foresaw when writing it had taken place and Brighton could be reached by train from London in 75 minutes.

Until Dr Richard Russell set up his practice in Brighthelmston (as it was then called) in 1754 and proclaimed the medicinal virtues of sea water, the place had been little more than a village. A contributor to the *Gentleman's Magazine* in 1766 described it as 'a small, ill-built town situated on the sea coast, at present greatly resorted to by persons labouring under various disorders for the benefit of bathing and drinking sea water, and by the gay and polite on account of the company that frequent it at that season.' He continued, sourly, that it had become 'one of the principal places in the kingdom for the resort of the idle and dissipated as well as of the diseased and infirm'. It was not until 1783 that the Prince Regent, later George IV, was recommended to take the cure at Brighton and fell in love with the place. Royal patronage gave it a new status if not precisely respectability.

The popularity of Brighton among wider circles of society began when peace followed the long years of war with Napoleon. Coaches vied with each other for custom and competed in speed. A six-hour journey from London was advertised as early as 1816, and passengers were offered a refund if time was not kept. Fifteen horses employed on the service died from their exertions in a week and the authorities stepped in. This was an age when any writer worthy of his salt could express himself in rhyming couplets and some of the verses which have survived give a lively impression of the period. In *Advice to Julia* (1821) Henry Luttrell recommends a trip to Brighton and portrays the bustling scene on the road:

'Starting each hour, ere day begins,
Till evening falls, from twenty inns,
Inside and out, a clustering load,
They spin along the level road;
That road which, oft curtailed, is passed

Each year more quickly than the last.
What crowds from each coach alight on
The russet Steyne and beach of Brighton.'

By 1822 there were 60 coaches daily between London and Brighton, 30 in each direction and the time for the journey had come down to between five and six hours as a result of new sections of road which shortened the distance. Brighton was building up its reputation for jollity for the work-weary. A contributor to *Blackwoods Magazine* in 1841, signing himself 'Arion', wrote:

'If you're sick of the earth
Take a twelve-shilling berth
On the roof of the fast coach, *The Triton*.
In five hours and a half
You shall sing, dance and laugh
In this Mahomet's paradise, – Brighton!'

Evidently Brighton was already celebrated for the grace and beauty of its *houris*. For further evidence one may go back to *Vanity Fair* and listen to Jos Sedley walking with companions on the sea front: 'What a monstrous fine girl that is in the lodgings over the milliner's! Gad, Crawley, did you see what a wink she gave me as I passed?'

Brighton was not all fun and frivolity, however. The town had been a packet port for Dieppe since the 18th century, and development of this business was a recurrent theme in the early years of the railway. Until the Chain Pier was opened in 1823 passengers had to be ferried to and from the packets in rowing boats. Witnessing the departure of the Dieppe packet was one of the diversions recommended to Julia by Henry Luttrell:

'Or pace along the shore remarking
A shoal of passengers embarking
(Well if they don't regret the step)
To join the packet for Dieppe.
Looking as grave as undertakers
(Their boat half swamped among the breakers)
Some sick, all terrified, in crossing
To where the distant bark lies tossing.'

Sea communications inspired one of the earliest proposals for a railway to Brighton. Shoreham, six miles west of Brighton was a natural harbour and a shipbuilding centre, but the shifting shingle bank that protected shipping from the open sea made the entrance

7

ill-defined and sometimes a navigational hazard. By the beginning of the 19th century it had silted up to such an extent that the harbour was of little use for commercial shipping. Work to improve the entrance was put in hand in 1816 and completed two years later. The *Brighton Herald* then reported that it was 'intended to lay down an iron railway from the point at which vessels discharge their cargoes to the western extremity of Brighton'. Communication with London, however, was to be by water by forming 'a junction of the Rivers Arun and Adur'. Nothing came of this proposal.

By the 1820s the steam locomotive was proving itself, and in 1823 a very early proposal for a railway between London and the Sussex Coast was put forward in a pamphlet published by William James. His idea, spelt out in the capitals characteristic of the period, was to connect 'the METROPOLIS with the ports of SHOREHAM (Brighton), ROCHESTER (Chatham) and PORTS-MOUTH by a line of ENGINE RAIL-ROAD.' He sought to show that by this means shares in a number of somewhat comatose undertakings, Shoreham Harbour among them, would become a 'productive property.' The map in his pamphlet showed the Sussex branch terminating a little to the east of Shoreham itself, approximately at Southwick, which was about the eastern limit of the harbour in those days.

James's ideas got no further than their airing in his pamphlet. Two years later an undertaking calling itself the Surrey, Sussex, Hants, Wilts & Somerset Railway Company employed John Rennie to survey routes from London to Brighton as part of the ambitious plans implied by its title. The company did not survive, but in later years one of the routes proposed by Rennie (by that time Sir John) was accepted as the main line of the London & Brighton Railway.

By the middle 1830s six projects for a railway between London and Brighton were under consideration by Parliament. Opinion in the town itself was divided between the various proposals, although generally in favour of a railway being built. On 27 July 1835 the Brighton Vestry (corresponding in those days to a Town Council) resolved that the establishment of a railway to London was 'highly expedient' and appointed a local committee to study the various schemes that were then engaging the attention of learned Counsel in the committee rooms at Westminster. The line via Henfield and Horsham proposed by Robert Stephenson found considerable support at first but met powerful opposition from the residents of aristocratic Brunswick Square who objected to having a railway terminus close to their houses. Stephenson had selected a site on the Western Road opposite the end of Waterloo Street, a short thoroughfare leading up from the sea front.

By the middle of 1836 opinion had veered to Rennie's line, called the 'direct' line, which was to terminate near Park Crescent at the back of the town. A public meeting in Brighton on 18 June in that year was decisively in favour and petitioned Parliament to reconsider its current apparent preference for Stephenson's line before a Bill was passed. Rennie's scheme made provision for branches to Shoreham, Lewes, and Newhaven. Stephenson would have put Shoreham on the main line but considered that a branch to Lewes and Newhaven would not pay for the cost of its maintenance. This was not in line with local opinion, which was already thinking of Brighton as a railway centre rather than simply a terminus.

The choice of line was still undecided at the beginning of 1837. On 25 January a Vestry meeting was addressed by spokesmen for the five concerns still in the field but the members were unmoved in their preference for the direct line and requested the two Members of Parliament for Brighton to convey to the House of Commons that the town considered the line to be 'of the utmost importance to the Town and at the same time productive of great national benefit.'

Even after the Parliamentary committee had voted in favour of the direct line there was a last minute hitch when Members for West Sussex who backed Stephenson's line sought to have the decision reconsidered. In Brighton the feeling now was that any line would be better than none and the Vestry agreed to a compromise proposal which adopted Stephenson's approach via Capel and Henfield but took the line to a terminus on the site selected by Rennie. In the meantime, however, the Government had decided that the arguments could not go on indefinitely and appointed an engineer of the Ordnance Department to report on the matter. The Vestry was alarmed at the prospect of more delay before a decision, but the Government engineer acted swiftly and pleased local opinion by giving his casting vote in favour of the 'direct line'. It had more constructional problems than Stephenson's line but better opportunities for branches and was seen as a single trunk route for the south from which other lines would radiate east and west into the rest of Sussex. The report was published in June 1837, and on 15 July in the same year the Bill for the London & Brighton Railway Company received the Royal Assent.

The London & Brighton Railway began at a junction with the London & Croydon Railway in Norwood, South London, near the present Norwood Junction. By using London & Croydon metals for the nine miles between the junction and London Bridge, only 41 miles 59 chains of new line had to be built to reach the coast at Brighton. Some 11¾ miles between the junction at Norwood and the present Redhill were in fact built jointly with the South Eastern Railway, whose trains also started from London Bridge but left the Brighton line at Redhill to continue eastwards over their own tracks to Folkestone and Dover.

The London & Brighton Railway Act also authorised the building of branches from Brighton to Shoreham, and to Lewes and Newhaven. Improvement of communications between Shoreham and Brighton had been urged since the building of the new harbour entrance in 1816. When John Vallance demonstrated his atmospheric railway system in Brighton, a resolution of the Brighton Vestry dated 5 June 1827 acknowledged that an atmospheric system conveying goods from Shoreham Harbour and passengers from London would be beneficial to the town. Vallance proposed to enclose the track in a continuous tunnel from which air could be exhausted ahead of the train to create a pressure difference between the two sides of a piston to which the train would be attached. Alternatively the pressure on one side of the piston could be raised above that of the atmosphere by compressors. It was claimed that with this system a train could be propelled at 100mph. A representative of the Russian Embassy who attended Vallance's demonstration was sufficiently impressed to recommend construction of an atmospheric line from St Petersburg to Moscow and the Black Sea. The Brighton Vestry contented itself with putting its interest on record in the minutes. Nobody came forward with financial backing and Vallance faded from the scene.

All but one of the proposed rail routes from London to Brighton had involved some tunnelling. The exception was the line suggested by Nicholas Cundy which would have branched from the London & Southampton Railway at Wandsworth and proceeded southwards by way of Leatherhead, Dorking, Horsham and Shoreham. It became known in Brighton as 'the London and Brighton Railway without a tunnel' but it dropped out of the competition at an early stage. Rennie's direct line had five tunnels, of which the two longest were at Merstham (1,831yd) through the North Downs and Clayton (2,259yd) through the South Downs. The forest ridge south of Crawley was pierced by a tunnel 1,133yd long near Balcombe.

Coal, freight and building materials in considerable quantities came to Brighton by sea. Until the harbour works at Shoreham were undertaken they were usually unloaded on to Brighton beach. The importance of the harbour to the town is seen in the fact that building of the Shoreham branch was begun at the same time as that of the main line but the Lewes and Newhaven branches were deferred.

Being under six miles long and without major engineering works, the Shoreham branch was completed first. It turned westward immediately on leaving Brighton station and entered a deep cutting, followed by a tunnel 231yd long before reaching the first station at Hove. The other intermediate stations were at Portslade, Southwick, Kingston, and Ham Common on the outskirts of Shoreham. Extension westwards seems to have been in prospect from the first for the layout of Shoreham station was not that of a conventional terminus with office buildings across the end of the line. The line was formally opened for passenger traffic on 11 May 1840, public services beginning on 12 May. On this occasion the *Brighton Herald* embellished its account of the proceedings with a number of engravings procured 'at great expense.' One of them shows Brighton station, which at that time seems to have been an unassuming structure not unlike an engine shed and less gracefully designed than the stone edifice supporting the water tank for supplying the locomotives. Construction of Mocatta's celebrated station building did not begin until October 1840.

The site on which the station was built was a little to the

THE TERMINUS AT BRIGHTON.

Above: **The Brighton Terminus – one of the engravings which illustrated the account of the opening of the Shoreham branch in the *Brighton Herald.** Madgwick Collection/Ian Allan Library (IAL)*

south of that originally proposed by Rennie. According to the *Brighton Herald* of 16 May 1840, 'the entrance to the Brighton terminus is at the top of Trafalgar Street where a very large space (bounded on the side nearest the town by a handsome wall) has been enclosed. The point is extremely central and when the approaches have been, as they must ultimately be, improved it will be found that no better spot could have been selected. The distance from North Street through Surrey Street is but a two or three minutes' walk.' Some more recent comments on the siting of Brighton station have been less complacent.

The station site was awkward from the civil engineering point of view. It was high up the western slope of the valley through which the London road entered the town, and the goods sidings on the eastern side of the station were actually 30ft below the level of the passenger lines. They were reached by a connecting line which left the Shoreham branch outside the terminus, the junction facing towards Shoreham, and descended to the lower level in a tunnel which passed under a corner of the station site.

Apart from the 'handsome wall' the only other architectural comment on the first station at Brighton was that 'a small building has been erected for the clerks.' The accommodation in the trains was clearly of greater interest. First class carriages were 'extremely handsome and fitted up in a style even of luxury.' The second class were 'not so expensively got up but for the intending traveller will be found to present every conveniency.' It was a different matter with the third class, which were of 'altogether rougher construction: the traveller must stand,

and take his chance, if there are many beside him, of being well hustled by his neighbours. They do not afford any protection from the rain.'

New England cutting, entered on leaving the terminus, struck the newspaper as 'a tremendous work as may be seen by the diminished appearance of the spectators who are looking down at the train as it rushes on.' Portslade was the half way point and here a shed for repairing engines had been provided. In those days the view from the line in this area was considered very picturesque, 'taking in the wide ocean on one side and the pleasant country on the other.'

At Kingston the line came very close to the main road, as it does today, and it was hoped that it would be 'a great convenience to the wharf owners who will be enabled to forward on their goods without delay, and at

Top: **Well-wishers at Brighton speed an inaugural train to Shoreham on its way into the New England Cutting – 'a tremendous work as may be seen by the diminished appearance of the spectators who are looking down at the train as it rushes on'.** *Madgwick Collection/IAL*

Above: **New England tunnel, 231yd long, approximately half way between Brighton and the original station at Hove.** *Madgwick Collection/IAL*

Right: **A train to Shoreham crosses Kingston Lane, leading to the wharves. Perhaps the steeply raked masts on the right represent a Dieppe Packet.** *Madgwick Collection/IAL*

THE VIADUCT AT KINGSTON.

less expense than hitherto.' The railway had its own wharf and sidings here, but there was a hitch in connecting them with the main line. To reach the wharf the track had to cross the road and the turnpike trustees objected. Although the railway advertised that it would convey goods and merchandise from Shoreham and Kingston as from 24 August 1840, traffic did not pass to and from the wharfside tracks until an uncertain date in July 1841, by which time agreement to lay the crossing had been reached. In later years the road was raised to cross the line on a bridge. The line to the wharves was connected with the layout on the inland side of the road by means of turntables.

The station at Shoreham was described as 'a long wooden shed with lodges for the clerks, on the same plans as the Brighton terminus.' From 27 June 1840 an omnibus service to and from Worthing connected with the trains at Shoreham station.

The arrival of the railway at Brighton was watched with interest on both sides of the Channel. Brighton had long-standing ties with Dieppe, perhaps because both towns were the nearest resorts on the open sea to their respective capitals, and in 1822 a regular steam packet service was introduced. The Chain Pier at Brighton was opened a year later to cater for the growing traffic to and from France. It avoided the previous uncomfortable transhipment to and from the beach. News items reporting the social scene and other matters in Dieppe were published week by week in the *Brighton Herald*. Early in 1840 the paper's Dieppe correspondent recorded that thoughts on that side of the Channel were turning towards better accommodation for the steamer passengers when both towns were served by rail. *La Vigie de Dieppe* complained of 'the very defective state of

the present steam navigation between this place and Brighton', and pressed the Municipal Council to 'co-operate with their ultra-marine neighbours in endeavouring to provide a packet more worthy of plying on this station.'

In Brighton it was feared that the Paris & Rouen Railway might not be continued to Dieppe. The *Brighton Herald* of 18 July 1840 wrote: 'To Brighton, with its railway, the construction of the Paris line to Dieppe is of the greatest importance since by stopping the line at Rouen the tide of passengers will be sent to Havre and so on by Southampton to the Metropolis.' The London & Southampton Railway had been opened throughout on 11 May 1840. It had its mishaps in the early days, which were reported with some relish in the Brighton press.

In the meantime the main line from London to Brighton was progressing southwards. It reached Haywards Heath on 11 July 1841. Passengers completed the journey by coach, the whole trip taking four hours. Some of the coaches employed had previously been running throughout between Brighton and London. New road services were put on between Haywards Heath, Lewes, Uckfield, Maresfield and Eastbourne in connection with the trains. The first journey over the line, reported the *Brighton Herald*, 'was performed in a manner to create the utmost confidence in its safety' and the paper forecast that 'the advantages of this great work will be felt in the remotest parts of the country.' Advantage was also expected across the Channel. The

Below: **David Mocatta's station building at Brighton.** *Brighton Public Libraries*

Herald's correspondent in Dieppe had expressed the hope that 'the partial opening of the railroad from London to Brighton on Monday will soon cause us to be crowded with fashionable visitants.'

By this time the new Brighton station designed for the railway by David Mocatta was complete. Tickets to watch the arrival of the first train from London were distributed widely, and those who saw the interior of the station for the first time were suitably impressed. Said the *Brighton Herald:*

'The aspect of the whole terminus – the light and wide-spread sheds which receive the trains, the spacious colonnades around the station house, and the numerous offices within this beautiful structure – was the general theme of admiration and fully occupied the attention of the company until the arrival of the expected train.'

Mocatta, who was not a Brighton Railway employee but had been commissioned by the company for architectural design, was responsible for the station house. The platform accommodation was the work of the company's engineer, John Rastrick. There were three overall roofs,

250ft long, one for the Shoreham line and two for the London lines. The roofs were constructed of wrought iron principals supported on cast iron columns and girders, boarded over and covered with slates. Brighton station has been admired for many years, but time has done much to obscure Mocatta's original work and the most striking feature today is the fine overall roof which was built above the old train sheds in 1882/3, Rastrick's structures being then dismantled. Mocatta's frontage was in a restrained Italianate style and in his day there were evidently some who preferred something more florid. The author of *The Rail Road Book of England* published in 1851 simply reported that 'the Brighton terminus, although not remarkable for architectural adornment, is a very commodious and convenient station.' Architecture

Fig 1. Brighton station and environs, 1846. The map, in Hove Public Library, on which this is based does not show the connection from the Shoreham line to the goods yard, but the area to the east of the terminus is labelled 'railway station'.

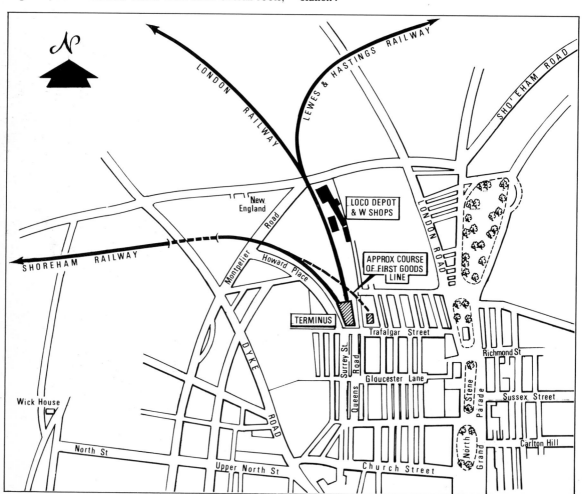

Left: The Wick Road viaduct on the main line approaching Brighton. Wick Road, named after one of the estates in the area which were sold for building land, was known later as Montpelier and then as New England Road. *Brighton Public Libraries*

Below: The Wick Road viaduct today. *Madgwick Collection/IAL*

apart, one must still marvel at the building of a great railway terminus on an artificial plateau 130ft above sea level which required the labour of 3,500 men and 570 horses. The station and its environs in the later 1840s are shown in Fig 1.

The best view of the proceedings on the opening day was not from within the station itself but was gained by the crowds who lined the slopes alongside the railway between the southern end of Patcham Tunnel and the station. A cloud of steam issuing from the tunnel mouth was the signal for a 'thousand cries of "here they come!"'. The next moment 'the long dark object was seen swiftly gliding along the line and rapidly increasing in size and distinctness as it approached, till, after being lost for a short time behind the curve, the first train from London came thundering along and receiving the hearty salutations of the crowds on the hill side, passed rattling over the viaduct*, passed the engine house, and was then lost to the sight of the external spectators as it turned round the rails to reach the terminus.'

Now the train first became visible to the crowds inside the station. One suspects that the Editor of the *Herald* was among them, for this account of the train's approach from Patcham came from a contributor and his own editorial comment was that 'the station house is certainly the worst point on the line for watching the approach of a train for the curve which the line takes round the hill on the left completely shuts out everything till the actual moment of arrival, when the speed is necessarily abated to the slowest possible point short of stoppage.'

*This was the Wick Road viaduct, said in an early guide to Brighton to have been 'designed after one of the Roman triumphal arches'. New England Road has replaced the old thoroughfare. Although overshadowed by the fame of the later London Road viaduct on the line to Lewes, it was considered a sufficiently august structure for its foundation stone to be laid on 27 May 1839, with full Masonic honours.

In welcoming the railway to Brighton, the Editor also reflected briefly on its effect on country towns and villages where trade had flourished in the coaching days, while a following leader, *Farewell to the Road!* dwelt nostalgically on coaching sights, sounds and characters under the sub-title 'Ichabod! Ichabod! The mighty are fallen!'

In the evening there was a banquet and speeches, with a lighter interlude half way through the proceedings described as 'Comic song by Mr Davies.' Brighton complimented the railway company, and the railway company complimented Brighton. John Rastrick, the railway's Engineer, recalled that the Mayor of Dieppe, visiting Brighton on a new steamship, was said to have described it as 'a town of palaces.' He himself called it the Queen of Watering Places. It is not clear whether he had invented the term on the spot or appropriated it from elsewhere. Many years later the writer of the official guide to the London, Brighton & South Coast Railway claimed it as a Brighton exclusive and deplored its frequent use by other resorts.

John Harman, Chairman of the London & Brighton Railway Company, touched on a subject that had caused some controversy. The railway reserved certain trains for first class passengers only. He explained that this was because 'The directors considered the traffic likely to come to this town a very superior traffic . . . they looked upon Brighton as inviting the most respectable, the highest families in the kingdom to come to it, and the directors had given accommodation to that class of person to travel to Brighton with the greatest comfort. They had accordingly adopted the plan of having first class trains, not with the object of wishing to shut out any persons who might wish to travel by them – far from it! – but with a view to benefit the town; for they had been led to believe that, without making a distinction, they might give umbrage to those persons who brought most wealth to the town.'

Harman was also hopeful of Continental traffic via Brighton. He had attended a meeting in the town at which proposals were explained for a floating breakwater to provide a harbour which vessels could enter and leave at all states of tide. One end of the eastern arm would have been attached to the Chain Pier. In applauding the idea, Harman hastened to add that the railway company could not provide the money for carrying it out, but he hinted that it could exert influence in useful places. Later, however, the directors agreed to contribute £300. Three sections of the breakwater were actually built and moored near the pier. The work went no further and after a year they were towed away to Shoreham Harbour, one section breaking away en route and being washed up on Brighton beach. There was another scheme in 1846 for a fixed breakwater which was enthusiastically supported by the Brighton Vestry, which considered that it would augment the traffic between England and France 'and bring into full operation the shortest and best route by Sea and Railway between London and Paris'. There is no record of construction having been begun. The London, Brighton & South Coast Railway developed Newhaven as its Continental port and Brighton did not get an artificial harbour until the present marina was opened in 1978.

As the London & Brighton Railway settled down to work the shareholders became dissatisfied with the Directors' conduct of the company's affairs and in 1843 the whole Board was voted out of office. Next but one in line to Harman as Chairman was Rowland Hill, temporarily discharged from the Post Office after a change of Government. Hill's ideas were less 'upmarket' than Harman's and he introduced excursion trains. The first ran on Easter Monday 1844. A new era in the history of Brighton had been launched and was graphically described in the *Brighton Herald*:

'During the first three days of the week it really seemed as if London had "precipitated itself" on Brighton so thick and fast did the living stream pour into our town. Thousands who never saw the Queen of Watering Places before seized the opportunity of doing so – hundreds gazed for the first time at the sea, not as they had seen it in grotesque miniature at Deptford or Woolwich but in the full extent of its grandeur and might as it rolls in from the boundless Atlantic.'

The 'monster train' as it was called was awaited by large crowds of spectators alongside the line inwards from Patcham, their curiosity mastering their impatience at its delayed arrival. A few minutes before twelve a bell was rung to announce that it had been sighted – one and a half hours late: 'Out-scouts who had caught a sight of it from elevated positions came hurrying down with prodigious reports of its vast extent and the crammed nature of its freight. Eyes were strained and necks stretched to catch a first sight of it; mothers caught up their little boys, young gentlemen seized the occasion to help their fair companions, tall men were intrusive, little men were desperate – everyone was eager to see the train come in!'

According to this account the train arrived with three locomotives but on some parts of its journey there had been four. It stopped outside the station and 'engines *Mars* and *Jupiter* went to the rear to push forward their huge load. It was worth near two hours' pushing and squeezing to see those 33 mortality-laden carriages black with life.'

Other accounts give it more carriages, but the *Herald* reporter said that the train with its three engines was 'just sufficient to fill up the space between the end of the cutting and the station – not less than 150 yards we should think.' Londoners were looked upon as an alien species and apart from those watchers who gathered to study them with sober curiosity there were some who had come avowedly to 'quiz the cockneys.' Even the reporter found entertainment as well as instruction in the

Right: **The Brighton Quadrille, a piece of music dedicated to the Brighton excursionist.** *Brighton Public Libraries*

VIEW OF BRIGHTON, FROM ROSE HILL NORTH.

THE BRIGHTON RAILROAD

QUADRILLES,

AND

Pavilion Waltz,

Composed for the Pianoforte,

& DEDICATED TO THE

VISITORS OF BRIGHTON,

BY

FREDᴷ WRIGHT.

Ent. Sta. Hall

Pr. 4/-

Published by

WRIGHT & SONS,

MUSIC SELLERS TO THE QUEEN, & MUSICAL INSTRUMENT DEALERS,

ROYAL COLONADE, BRIGHTON.

spectacle. 'It was an amusing sight enough' he wrote ' to watch the stream that now flowed out of the station doors and to note the new class of visitors whom the railway had introduced for the first time into Brighton. On such occasions, however, criticism would be ill-natured. The arrivals were of a quiet, respectable class whom it was not difficult to recognise as they strolled about the town.'

After 1,000 passengers on the first train, 500 more came on a second. It was reckoned that over the three days of the holiday nearly 10,000 persons must have entered the town. *The Times* noticed the event and unkindly hinted that the London & Brighton Railway had not been alone in taking customers for a ride – some Brighton traders and landladies had joined in with enthusiasm. This was hotly denied with the assertion that the visitors had been offered 'board and lodging of the best and most economical description.'

Brighton residents enjoyed cheap fares to London and 'great numbers availed themselves of the liberality of the Railway Directors to make a trip to the metropolis. Over the three days of the holiday the up trains took 2,500 on Monday, 1,200 on Tuesday, and between 3,000 and 4,000 on Wednesday, when the last train was composed of no less than 36 carriages containing above 1,100 persons.'

The days when 'the quality' came to Brighton by carriage or coach, to be greeted on arrival by a 'Master of Ceremonies' were coming to an end, although that official retained his post until 1854. Brighton's social 'Season' shifted to the end of the year, the town being taken over by 'the Masses' from June to October. Local traders welcomed this extension of the time during which Brighton was thronged with visitors. The ease of access from London also promoted a new 'industry' in the town. It became the fashion among the well-to-do to send children to school at Brighton, and by 1851 there were said to be 189 private schools in the town. Perhaps Dr Blimber's Academy in *Dombey and Son* is Dickens' portrait of an early specimen.

From now on there would be two Brightons; the Brighton of Royal Crescent, Sussex Square and the Pavilion on one hand, and on the other the Brighton that in due course would become known as 'between the piers.' Here the palmists and the souvenir stalls would flourish unperturbed by passing time while side by side with them the vendors of Brighton Rock, ice cream, bubble gum, candy floss, and hamburgers would keep pace with the changing tastes of the consumer society. In his book *Brighton: Its history, its foibles and its fashions*, Lewis Melville summed up the situation thus in 1909.

'The short distance that separates it (Brighton) from London, which was one of the primary causes of its popularity in the coaching days, has, since the advent of the railways, proved itself an element destructive of its exclusiveness. Cheap excursions for "trippers" and half-guinea Pullman Car trains for the well-to-do, have changed the character of the place out of all recognition. Brighton has developed into the Cockney's paradise, the Mecca of the stockbroker and the chorus-girl.'

Below: **Bank Holiday Monday, 1872, at Brighton, and locomotives wait to take returning excursions. The building on the right is the paint shop of Brighton Works, which was moved to this position from the east side of the line by Stroudley. It was converted for the maintenance of electric rolling stock in the 1930s.** *Madgwick Collection/IAL*

2. The Steam Years – Expanding the Service

For some six years after the opening of the main line to Brighton the railway handled Continental traffic there and at Shoreham. Steamers operated by the General Steam Navigation Company sailed from Shoreham Harbour to Dieppe, mostly calling at Brighton's Chain Pier to embark and land passengers although services direct from Shoreham to Dieppe were also advertised. The calls at the Chain Pier were 'weather permitting' and so Kingston station on the Shoreham branch must often have seen Continental passengers passing through. In fact, the London & Brighton Railway's own advertisement stating that 'The quickest route to Paris is by the railway to Shoreham and thence by packet to Dieppe' suggests that the transfer between train and boat was made as often at Kingston Wharf as at Brighton. In 1843 it was announced that if the steamer from Dieppe arrived at Shoreham too late for passengers to connect with the 6.30pm train from Brighton to London, a special through train for London would be despatched from Kingston.

In 1844 through carriages between London and Shoreham were introduced for first class passengers, most of them by trains which stopped at Kingston. These would have been useful for passengers by the sailings from Kingston Wharf to Le Havre, which did not call at Brighton. Second and third class passengers could use the same trains but had to alight at Brighton to join the Shoreham or London train while the first class coaches were being shunted between the main line and west coast line platforms.

In 1847 the railway formed a subsidiary company to operate its own ships. Differences arose with the Shoreham Harbour authorities and the passenger services were transferred to Newhaven. From 1841 to 1843 Brighton and Shoreham had been the only rail-served Channel packet stations but in the latter year the South Eastern Railway reached Folkestone and co-operated with a shipping company in a day service to Boulogne.

Apart from its Continental ambitions the London & Brighton Railway seemed content to act within the limits defined by its title and showed little disposition to build the Lewes and Newhaven branches as it was empowered

Below: **Shoreham Station in 1870.** *Madgwick Collection/IAL*

Left: The original station building at Worthing illustrated here was saved from demolition in 1971 by the Department of the Environment, being listed as 'of historic and architectural interest'. *Stephen Goodger*

Below: A modern view of Worthing Station shows the old building still intact on the left, although development work is creeping up to it. *John Scrace*

Right: An early print of Brighton station west side. *National Railway Museum, Crown Copyright*

to do. Local companies were responsible for the extensions westward and eastward that converted Brighton from a railway terminus into a railway centre. Two such companies were formed in 1844, and the Acts of both empowered them to sell their lines to the London & Brighton.

The first new line to open was an extension from Shoreham to Worthing built by the Brighton & Chichester Railway Company. L&B trains began running over the line on 24 November 1845. By this time excitement over new railways was waning. The opening attracted little attention in Brighton and a celebration dinner at the Nelson Inn in Worthing was 'not very numerously attended.' There was a mishap during the day when a team of horses hauling ballast from Upper to Lower Lancing for laying a second track was alarmed by the approach of the 12.50 train from Worthing and bolted. One of the horses was struck by the locomotive and killed. The locomotive was derailed but 'all passengers escaped with a fright and a shock, except one gentleman, who received a contusion of the knee.' Several passengers in a train from Brighton to Worthing which was delayed by the derailment chose to alight and walk the last three miles to their destination, the ladies among them being observed to step out briskly through the cold but bright November afternoon.

The Shoreham branch was now merged with a main line which was pressing westwards along the coast to Portsmouth, for the Brighton & Chichester company had already been authorised to extend. Portsmouth was reached on 14 June 1847, in time for special excursions to be run between Portsmouth and Brighton on 26, 27 and 28 June for 'the Holiday in Celebration of Her Majesty's Coronation' (it was, in fact, the 10th anniversary).

Construction of the Lewes branch from Brighton was undertaken by the Brighton, Lewes & Hastings Railway Company. Its opening on 8 June 1846 coincided with

that of the extension of the west coast line from Worthing to Chichester. Trains to both places left Brighton at about 7 o'clock, close to the time of a departure for London. The *Brighton Herald* commented that 'the appearance of the three trains, thus about to carry their passengers at the same moment east, west, and north, was very lively.' This liveliness was not reflected at Lewes, where 'nothing was done to celebrate the occasion; for a portion of the inhabitants are in dudgeon about their stations.' There was a partial boycott of the trains, some of the stage coaches being kept running with the support of the malcontents.

A letter from a Lewes tradesman set out the complaints. It was claimed that a promise to consult the interests of the town as a whole as to where the station should be had not been kept; and that instead of building a direct line from St Marys Lane to Southerham a deviation had been made through the property of one of the directors. The line to Hastings* left the deviation with a curve 'of an apparently fearful character.' The people of Lewes had been appeased by the promise that they should have 'a substantial station house' erected for their accommodation. The indignant correspondent concluded: 'If a roofless shed, having the appearance of a cow-house, be a *substantial station house*, then have the directors fulfilled their pledge, but not otherwise.'

Other things apart, the original arrangements at Lewes were inconvenient for through traffic between Brighton and Hastings for the station was a terminus and trains calling there had to be propelled out before proceeding on their way eastward round the 'fearsome curve.' Platforms were provided, however, at Ham (also called Southover) on the line to Hastings which enabled the town to be served without entering the terminus, but they were further from the centre.

*The line then terminated at St Leonards. The section onwards to Hastings was built by the South Eastern Railway and opened to the traffic of both companies in 1851.

Above: **The viaduct across the Preston Road in Brighton is today generally called the London Road viaduct. Built for the branch to Lewes opened in 1846, it was the genesis of the east coast line. This engraving shows the early works buildings and the main line to London in the right background, but the junction appears to face in the wrong direction.** *Brighton Public Libraries*

Above right: **The artist of this view of the London Road viaduct, drawn for the *British Gazetteer,* shows the portal of 'Ditchling Tunnel' (only 63yd long) in the background. London Road station was built between the end of the viaduct and the tunnel.** *Madgwick Collection/IAL*

Right: **The arches reconstructed after bomb damage are conspicuous in this view of the viaduct from the south side.** *G. Daniels*

Shortly after the line was opened from Brighton to Lewes a Bill to amalgamate the London & Brighton and the London & Croydon Railway Companies received the Royal Assent on 27 July 1846. The combined undertaking was called the London, Brighton & South Coast Railway. It was an appropriate title for the company's tracks already extended along the South Coast from Chichester in the west to St Leonards in the east, the Lewes-St Leonards section having been opened on 27 June in that year. Brighton was the focal point, all traffic to and from the eastern and western coastal sections having to pass through it.

The line to Lewes brought a new and now familiar landmark to the Brighton scene. It diverged eastward from the main line a short distance outside the station and at once crossed the valley on a viaduct 400yd long with 27 arches of which 11 are built on a curve of 10ch radius and 16 on a curve with a radius of three-quarters of a mile. Curvature and height – at the centre it is 67ft above the ground – combine to make the structure both graceful and impressive. The longest span, of 50ft, crosses the road to London and the structure today is known as the London Road viaduct, but when it was built the same thoroughfare was called Preston Road and early accounts refer to it as the Preston viaduct. Ten million bricks were used in its construction, which occupied only 10 months from laying the first stone to keying the last arch.

Some contemporary local opinion found the viaduct less admirable than later generations have done. The attitude was summed up by the *Brighton Herald* thus:

'Some objections have been urged against this viaduct. The principal one is the expense; the second is liability to be blown up by an enemy. To the first it may be replied that the saving in expense by an embankment would not have compensated for the damage done to the adjoining property and the injury to the town. To the second, that if an enemy got within gun-shot range of the viaduct other works such as the terminus itself and the workshops with their stock of engines and carriages would be more likely to suffer than the solid fabric of the viaduct.'

In the England of 1846 an enemy attack on the viaduct may have seemed improbable, but less than a hundred years later, in May 1943, it suffered a direct hit in a low-level raid by six Focke-Wulfe fighter bombers and two arches were damaged. They were repaired with such speed and energy that vital freight traffic was crossing again within 24 hours.*

On the outskirts of Brighton the line crossed the Lewes road on a skew bridge of three brick arches of 60ft span, similar in construction to those of the viaduct. The bridge was considered of sufficient interest to be illustrated by engravings in the local press and it is still a distinctive structure.

The Brighton Vestry showed much interest in the coastal lines, adding its voice to those of other petitioners during the passage of the various Bills. The lines brought trade to Brighton from two directions and at that time all traffic between the coastal routes and the London main line had to pass through the town. There was some uneasiness that the situation might not last, but the Vestry pinned its hopes on the eventual creation of a continuous railway from Dover to Portsmouth which would not be under the control 'of the South Western or any other company interested in obstructing the coast line and diverting the traffic to other lines in which they are more interested.' These hopes were dashed when the South Eastern Railway persuaded Parliament that it could provide a better service from London to Hastings via

*See also Appendix 2.

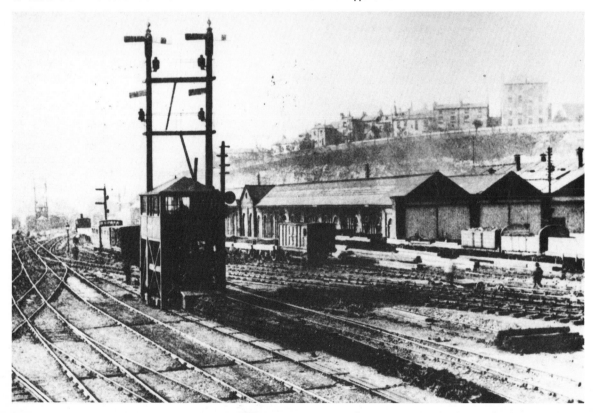

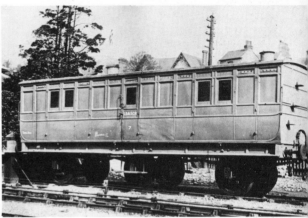

Ashford than the LBSC could via Lewes and was authorised to build a Hastings-Ashford line connecting at Ashford with its main line to Dover.

Brighton did not long remain the pivot point for all traffic to and from the coast lines. On 2 October 1847 the LBSC opened a cut-off from Keymer Junction, near Wivelsfield on the London main line, to Lewes, enabling trains from London for the east coast section to avoid Brighton. The branch from Lewes to Newhaven was opened on 8 December of the same year. Traffic from London for Chichester and Portsmouth continued to be routed via Brighton station until a more direct route via Three Bridges and Horsham became available with the opening of the Mid-Sussex Junction line on 3 August 1863.

Rennie's 'direct' line favoured journeys between Brighton and London rather than the inland towns of Sussex and those on its borders. Crawley and Horsham were served by a branch from Three Bridges opened on 14 February 1848 and extended to Petworth on 19 October 1859. The later through service between Brighton and Horsham via Shoreham did not begin until 16 September 1861 when a branch from Shoreham to

Partridge Green which had been opened on 1 July of that year was extended to join the Petworth-Shoreham line at Itchingfield Junction (see Chapter 6).

To the east of the main line, rail communication between Brighton and East Grinstead was established on 9 July 1855 with the opening of a branch from Three Bridges. The route via Lewes and Horsted Kenyes was not completed until 1 August 1882. Tunbridge Wells was also first reached from Brighton via Three Bridges, the East Grinstead branch being extended to Groombridge and Tunbridge Wells on 1 October 1866. Again a route via Lewes followed, the final section being completed on 3 August 1868. These lines were built by private companies which were taken over later by the LBSC. They provided pleasant meanders through rural inland Sussex, the flavour of which can be recaptured today on the Bluebell Railway between Horsted Kenyes and Sheffield Park, a preserved portion of the Lewes-East Grinstead line. Services from London today over what remains of them do not penetrate south of Uckfield.

On the main line to London the general pattern of service in the early days was six trains each way, one or two of which were first class only. The others, described as mixed trains, were first and second class. In the original time-table a first class train from Brighton at 8.30am ran to London Bridge in 1¾hr, calling only at Croydon. It was soon slowed to 2hr and made additional stops but a fast morning service to London was to reappear in various forms over the years, culminating in the celebrated 'City Limited'.

Top: **A 'Jenny Lind' 2-2-2 built in 1847 by E. B. Wilson.** *IAL*

Above: **The bridge over Trafalgar Street at Brighton station.**
National Railway Museum

Right: **An improved 'Jenny Lind' 2-2-2, seen in its later years after rebuilding by Stroudley and being named** *Southsea.*
Madgwick Collection/IAL

The mixed trains called at all stations and took 2½hr. In 1842 third class carriages were attached to one goods train in each direction. The timings were unattractive. Departures from each terminus were at 9am and arrival in London or Brighton at 12.45am. The 1843 timetable again saw first class trains running between Brighton and London in 1¾hr, this time with two stops, and third class passengers were now admitted to certain stopping trains. Third class facilities tended to be changed and curtailed at the whim of the railway and in 1848 the Brighton Vestry took up the cudgels on behalf of the third class passenger. A letter reminded the railway company that: 'Property has its duties as well as its rights and that in the adjustment of these principles the labouring and poorer classes of Society have a right to be considered especially in the management of Monopolies regulated by Act of Parliament.' As is usual in such disputes today, the protesters asserted that more trains and still lower fares would promote the interests of the shareholders themselves, while the railway replied that in its view the benefits to the shareholders had been very small while those to the town had been very great. The number of third class trains had been reduced because they had been 'found to be used by a class of person for whom they were not intended.'

In 1844 the best time from Brighton to London came down to 1½hr, with one stop. This was the schedule of the 8.45am up, while the corresponding down train at 4.40pm from London Bridge did the journey with the same stop (Redhill) in 1hr 35min. Both trains were first class only.

At this time work was in progress on improving the approach from the town to Brighton station by building the present Queens Road, which by continuing the line of West Street gives a straight run up from the front, past the Clock Tower, to the station forecourt. The railway contributed £2,000 to the work and also undertook construction of a bridge over Trafalgar Street which enlarged the station forecourt and improved access from the new road. If the local authorities were sometimes irritated by the railway's fares policy and timetables, the parties co-operated in other respects and when, after a long dispute over ownership of the grandstand on Brighton Racecourse, the building was bought by the town for £360, the railway contributed £100 towards the purchase. In 1853 the LBSC Directors contributed 50 guineas to the founding of the Brighton Regatta. A further example of railway benevolence at a later date was free conveyance for children of the Industrial Schools in Brighton to Shoreham for a school treat at the Swiss Gardens organised by the Brighton Board of Guardians.

The London & Brighton Railway began life with a fleet of 31 locomotives from various builders, but in 1844 these were put into a common pool with locomotives of the London & Croydon and South Eastern Railways. This arrangement came to an end in 1846, the

locomotives being divided between the London & Brighton (with which the London & Croydon was about to merge) and the South Eastern. In this share-out the L&B received 51 locomotives. Most of the passenger engines were of the 2-2-0 or 2-2-2 wheel arrangement, and among the first new orders placed for what had now become the London, Brighton & South Coast Railway was one for nine 2-2-2s designed by David Joy for the railway's requirements and built by E. B. Wilson & Company. The first locomotive was named *Jenny Lind,* and so 'Jenny Linds' became the class name for the locomotives subsequently built to the same design for a number of railways. In responding to the needs of the Brighton line, Joy created one of the classic locomotive designs of the early period. Individuality came to Brighton locomotives later when the company opened its own works in the town. Up to then the locomotives bought outside had been adapted as necessary.

Early observers of the railway scene were rarely explicit about details of locomotives and rolling stock. The description of the first train to Brighton as 'a long, dark object . . . swiftly gliding along the line,' which has been quoted already, leaves much to be filled in by the imagination. The reporter who noted the locomotives *Mars* and *Jupiter* fussing about in the approaches to Brighton station with the first excursion from London was unusually observant. These were 2-2-2 engines built by Sharp, Roberts and numbered 10 and 11 in the original London & Brighton stock. The breed is generally known as 'Sharpies.'

In spite of John Harman's short spell of office as first Chairman of the London & Brighton Railway his ideas on the importance of first class traffic evidently took root. Season tickets to London, introduced in 1845, were at first available to first class travellers only. An annual ticket between Brighton and London Bridge then cost £50, and was later reduced to £40. The timings of the morning up and evening down first class business trains were improved on several occasions. The up train was made non-stop in 75min in 1856 and by this time there were further first class only trains during the day for the more leisured traveller. At summer weekends extra trains ran from London to Brighton on Saturday afternoons and back again on Monday mornings, while for the day

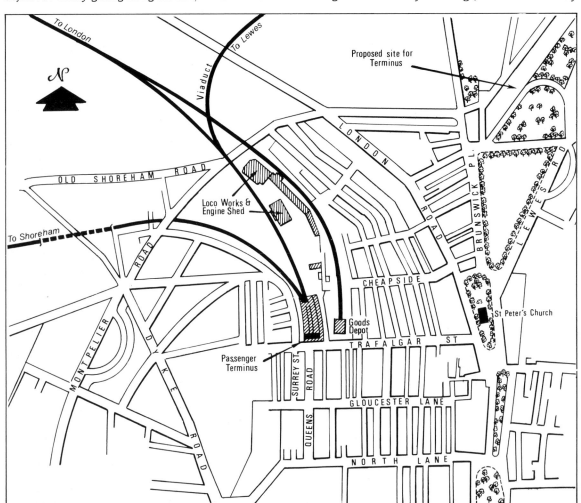

Above: **A 'B1' ('Gladstone' class) 0-4-2 heads a London-Worthing through train on the Cliftonville Curve (Preston Park to Hove, avoiding Brighton Station).**
Madgwick Collection/IAL

Fig 2. Building in Brighton spreads north with the coming of the railway (cf the map in Fig 1, Chapter 1). The period is 1853 and the connection from the London line to the goods station is shown, while the word 'goods' has been prominently added to the 'railway station' of the earlier map. *Based on a map in Brighton Public Library.*

tripper there were London-Brighton excursions on Sundays for five shillings (25p) third class. Outside the crack business trains the timings of the ordinary Brighton 'fasts' were not exciting. In 1856 they were taking 1hr 50min for the 50½ miles. Of the 12 down trains in that year three were first, second and third, six first and second and three first class only. In the up direction only two trains conveyed third class passengers. Fig 2 shows Brighton station environs in 1853, including a new approach to the goods station (see also Chapter 6).

The year 1858 was important in the development of the main line service for the line from Norwood Junction to the Crystal Palace was extended to Battersea and trains began running to this new West End terminus on 29 March. In 1860 Battersea was connected with Victoria station, which was used regularly by Brighton trains from 1 October. Trains conveying portions to or from Victoria and London Bridge divided or combined at East Croydon. The cut-off line from Windmill Bridge junction, Croydon, to Balham, avoiding Norwood Junction, was opened in December 1862 and this became the normal route for trains between Brighton and Victoria. It reduced the distance from Brighton by about two miles compared with running via Norwood Junction and put it on a par

with that to London Bridge. The railway map south of London was taking its familiar shape. In 1868 the opening of the South Eastern Railway's cut-off line from New Cross to Tonbridge relieved the congested Brighton line of some SER traffic, although secondary services from London to Tonbridge continued to travel via Redhill for many years.

There were also changes in Brighton itself. After the Mid-Sussex line had by-passed the town for London-Portsmouth trains, London-Worthing trains continued to run into Brighton station, reversing there to continue their journey along the west coast line. Residents of Worthing and of Brighton's growing neighbour resort of Hove were critical of the time wasted by this procedure. In 1875, therefore, the LBSCR obtained powers to build a curve from the London main line at Preston to a junction in Hove with the west coast line. Preston was a village on the London road about a mile and a half north of Brighton. A station was opened there on 1 November 1869 to cater for traffic from new residential development. Soon the village was lost among highly desirable residences whose occupants could enjoy living by the sea while keeping at a decent distance from the pier, the boarding houses, and the amusements.

The new curve, which passed through a tunnel 535yd long, was opened on 1 July 1879. It joined the coast line a little distance east of Cliftonville station. Cliftonville was a housing development extending eastward from the old village of Hove; its station had been opened on 1 October 1865. When the Cliftonville curve was opened, however, Cliftonville station was renamed West Brighton. This was not simply geographical. A West Brighton Estate Company had been set up in 1872 and was responsible for the long, wide avenues leading from the sea front towards the Downs which are characteristic of present-day Hove. This area was, in fact, the fastest growing part of Hove in the 1870s and 1880s.

In the year the curve was opened the old Hove station at the top of Holland Road, dating from the original Shoreham branch, was closed and converted into a goods yard. For some years the name of Hove was absent from the timetables, but on 1 October 1894 West Brighton was renamed Hove & West Brighton. 'West Brighton' was dropped a year later and it has been Hove station ever since.

In his book of Brighton reminiscences, *A peep into the past* (1892), J. G. Bishop recalled the effect on traffic of the Cliftonville curve. The old Cliftonville station had seen 'only a few straggling passengers making their way by newly formed roads or through the fields to their houses in the sparse neighbourhood.' In a few years' time, however, every train at West Brighton was 'discharging its long stream of passengers to a largely-builded district'. There was a similar growth in activity at Preston, renamed Preston Park when the curve was opened, which had been 'so metamorphosed of late to adapt it to the requirements of the West Brighton junction that it bears no resemblance whatever to the original station.' The 'metamorphosis' had included the replacement of the old up and down platforms with two

Left: The first engine named *Hove* was this Kitson 2-4-0, which was awarded a gold medal when exhibited in Paris in 1867 and subsequently bought by Craven. It is shown as modified by Stroudley, but the cab style still suggests that the builder had export orders in mind. *Madgwick Collection/IAL*

Centre left: Preston Park station still has the two island platform layout which it acquired when the Cliftonville Curve was opened. *John Scrace*

Below: Hove station today. The old station building is on the left, adjacent to the westbound platform. Trains from London via the Cliftonville curve can run into that platform or into the outer face of the island. *British Rail*

Below right: A modern view of the old station building at Hove, opened in 1866 and then called Cliftonville. *British Rail*

new islands, one for Brighton trains and the other for those taking the curve. At the same time an extra down line was brought into use between Brighton and Preston Park.

At West Brighton (ex-Cliftonville) the up platform was made an island. Trains to Brighton or Preston Park used the inner face. Down trains coming off the curve could either run into the down coast line platform or take a down loop line which served the outer face of the island, joining the down coast line west of the station. West Brighton, Shoreham and Worthing were served from London both by through trains and by through coaches on London-Brighton trains, sometimes detached at Preston Park and sometimes slipped there, or at Horley or Haywards Heath. Slipping had been practised on the LBSCR since 1858.

Even when J. Pearson Pattinson was writing *British Railways* in 1893 the third class service was open to criticism. He commented:

'Brighton itself is very badly off, the fastest down taking 75 minutes (70 minutes on Saturday nights) and the fastest up 73 minutes. This is not so good as it looks as all the other third class trains are longer on the journey, and the up service is distinctly worse than the down.'

He found the third class, and even the second class carriages 'in nearly all cases much inferior to the northern lines.' However, some thirds built specially for main line services were 'really excellent.' But these were exceptions 'for many of the thirds are without cushions of any kind, and except when the carriage is an open one throughout, the compartments are often stuffy and of small capacity.'

Brighton station underwent changes on several occasions to adapt to the expanding train service. At first capacity was increased by lengthening platforms. When

this was done in 1853 the extension of platforms beyond the train shed roofs resulted in the junction between the west coast line and the main line occurring within the platform length, as can still be seen today. Another continuing reflection of earlier times is the Middle Siding between Platforms 2 and 3 in the present station. This was the exit from the steam shed after it was moved into the angle between the west coast and main lines and locomotives coming off shed could stand there without occupying platform space before moving off to their trains. From the adjacent Platform 3 there was access to all three routes out of the station, but the position of the crossover to the west coast line on this platform road restricted the length of train that could be handled without division and shunting.

Further developments in the early 1860s included new platforms and a new main arrival line to serve them. Improvements to the layout in the station approaches made it necessary to carry more tracks across the New England Road. The new girder bridge at this point came in for some criticism locally on the grounds that it would 'by its darkness and damp ruin this end of the town, spoil the view, harbour pickpockets, and frighten the horses of those burgesses who liked to drive their lady friends along what was once a pleasant country road.' By the 1870s the layout in the station approaches was as shown in Fig 5.

The rebuilding that gave the station its present aspect took place in 1882/3. It then acquired its famous roof in two main curved spans, wide-arched and elliptical in form. The openwork decoration of beams and spandrels is elaborate, and the roof is supported by unusually tall and slender iron columns. Externally, however, the arched roof supports the sloping sides of a pitched roof or triangular section so that the impression from the end view is of gables. The LBSC's civil engineer responsible

Left: **The present entrance to Hove Station, built in 1904.** *British Rail*

Centre left: **The early roofing over the Brighton platforms.** *National Railway Museum, Crown Copyright*

Below: **The north end of Brighton Station about 1870, before construction of the present roof.** *Madgwick Collection/IAL*

Right: **Brighton station during erection of the new roof.** *National Railway Museum, Crown Copyright*

Centre right: **Brighton station interior after the rebuilding of 1882/3. Locomotives are seen standing on the 'middle road' on the right.** *Bucknall Collection/IAL*

Below: **Brighton station north end after the 1882/3 rebuilding. Note the 'arrival' signals with a distant arm which was left 'on' if a train was entering a partly occupied platform.** *Madgwick Collection/IAL*

Left: **The 'porte cochère' and Trafalgar Street bridge at Brighton about 1903.** *National Railway Museum, Crown Copyright*

Top: **First class bogie coach.** *Madgwick Collection/IAL*

Above: **Main line bogie composite.** *Madwick Collection/IAL*

for the rebuilding was F. D. Banister, but the roof itself was the work of H. E. Wallis. The clock suspended over the concourse dates from this time.

By this time no room remained on the station site for extra platforms and more capacity had to be gained by lengthening some of those already existing. By this means two trains of medium length could be handled in one platform. Each platform used in this way had an arrival signal with stop and distant arms. When the track was clear to the buffers both arms were pulled 'off', but if another train or even a single vehicle were already at the platform the distant arm remained 'on' and the driver of an arriving train had to proceed with great caution.

Another feature of the rebuilding was the erection of an awning, or *porte cochère,* along the front and east wall of the station building and out over the forecourt where it bridged Trafalgar Street. This was a practical arrangement for passengers arriving by cab, or in their own transport, but at the same time as it protected them from bad weather (as it still does) it spoiled the view of Mocatta's station house.

In its final stage of steam age development Brighton station (then known as Brighton Central) had 11 platforms, numbered from west to east. Platforms 1 and 2 served west coast line trains, and as has been seen there was access from Platform 3 to the west coast, main, and

Left: **Brighton South signalbox.**
Madgwick Collection/IAL

Below: **Interior of the South box.** *By courtesy of Mr Peter Hay*

Left: **Signal gantry at the approach to the station. Each post carries main and shunt signals for both directions of running and there are route indicators on the gantry itself.** *Madgwick Collection/IAL*

Right: **Brighton motive power depot in R. J. Billinton's day. The three locomotives in the centre of the front row are, from left to right: Class D3 0-4-4T No 397,** *Bexhill;* **Class G 2-2-2 No 343,** *Wilmington;* **and Class B1 0-4-2 No 214,** *Gladstone.* *IAL*

east coast lines, but at no time have connections between the three routes in the station been easy, and as late as 1926 the LBSC was seeking powers to build a south to west curve near Preston Park. A more radical proposal in the Beeching 'reshaping' era was to build a new Brighton station north of the present site, laid out as a through station instead of a terminus; all Victoria-Portsmouth trains would have been routed through Brighton, and the Mid-Sussex line closed.

Prior to electrification Platform 4 was a bay between Platforms 3 and 5 and was used by steam push-pull trains on the main line stopping service between Brighton and Haywards Heath. Platforms 10 and 11 were also used for auto-trains, but also for east coast line services, with No 11 primarily for the Kemp Town branch. Passenger traffic in the station was controlled by the West signalbox (120 levers), the South signalbox (240 levers), and Montpelier signalbox (98 levers), the last-named controlling the junction between the east coast and main lines. There were several other boxes in the Brighton area (Fig 9), and in 1926 the Brighton stationmaster was responsible for 10 in all.

A description of Brighton motive power depot published in 1913 gave the dimensions of the main shed as 158ft long and 201ft wide, with 14 roads inside. Between this building and the running lines there was a separate shed 483ft long and 50ft wide with three roads. This was equipped at the time as a washing out shed, but

in the 1920s it was known as the New Shed and used for preparing locomotives for their duties. The roads entered the shed at the station end and emerged at the country end, continuing to connect with the lines into the station. Locomotives when ready for service were parked on these tracks until the time came for them to join their trains. They were arranged in order of their departures and were despatched one after the other to run forward over the points and then back on to their coaches in the main line platforms. The main shed had no outlet at the country end and locomotives proceeding direct from there to their duties had to back into the station first before shunting on to their trains. After electrification the New Shed was abandoned and in its final years was used for motor vehicle maintenance, foreshadowing one of the functions of the engineering departments' establishment which later occupied the whole of the motive power depot site. Locomotives needing to be turned did not have to enter the yard. There was also a turntable between the main and east coast lines at Montpelier junction.

An account of Brighton station published in 1926 recorded that 7 million passengers arrived and departed in a year, of whom 5 million were handled in the summer months. The total in an average Sussex Fortnight (Bank Holiday week and the week before) might be over 1¼ million. Average daily train arrivals and departures in the summer were 218 in and 216 out. At holiday periods

ENTRANCE TO CLAYTON TUNNEL.

such as Easter, Christmas and the August Bank Holiday over 500 trains might have to be handled in a day.

Brighton suffered one of the classic railway accidents of the 19th century. It occurred in Clayton Tunnel, 4¾ miles from the terminus on the main line to London, where the railway burrows under the South Downs. Shortly after 8 o'clock on the morning of 25 August 1861 three trains left Brighton in quick succession. The first was from Portsmouth, and on entering the tunnel it failed to reset at danger an automatic signal protecting it in the rear. An excursion train from Brighton was hard on its heels, and as the signal was still falsely showing clear the signalman at the Brighton end of the tunnel waved a red flag to stop it. Braking hard, the driver brought his train to a standstill inside the tunnel, out of sight of the signalman. Fearing that it had failed to stop, the man telegraphed his colleague at the northern end of the tunnel to ask if the train had passed him. A fatal confusion now occurred. The signalman at the northern end replied that the train had passed, but he meant the Portsmouth train. Unhappily the signalman at the south portal took the reply to mean that the Brighton train had cleared the tunnel. A stopping train from London was by now approaching rapidly, and the signalman admitted it to the tunnel on the assumption that the line was clear. In the collision which followed 23 persons were killed and 175 injured. The disaster focused attention on the weaknesses of the time interval system of despatching trains. Departures from Brighton were supposed to be at not less than 5min intervals, but with traffic running late on this occasion the rule had not been observed.

Contemporary accounts build up a graphic picture of events in Brighton on that summer Sunday morning. There was anxiety at the station when trains due from London failed to arrive, then incredulity, turning to horror as the first reports came back from Clayton. The news spread like wildfire through the town. From the streets it percolated into the churches and chapels, where morning services were being held. There was whispering and commotion in the pews near the doors. Vergers frowned and shook their heads in reproof, then when they learned what had occurred hastened up the aisles and whispered discreetly to the clergy. Some nimble-witted Ministers, we are told, 'took occasion to make some edifying remarks on the catastrophe to their respective congregations'.

By mid-morning local newspapers had special editions on the streets. In the following week one editor took a rival to task for 'showing more appreciation of acquisitiveness than decorum in making the time of issuing his supplement coincident with the occurrence of Divine worship in the Chapel next door to his office . . . the disturbance was such as to seriously interfere with devotion, and the sermon was strangely interpolated with whistling cries of "Ere you are – only tuppence", with the *gamins* of the town having taken advantage of the demand to advance cent per cent upon the publishing price of the precious document'. It may be suspected that the critic had been slower off the mark than his competitor in getting his special issue off the press.

A train brought the bodies of victims back to the station for identification, where a library and reading room had been made ready. Readers of the local press got their full two-pennyworth in the reporters' descriptions of the harrowing scenes and the nature of the injuries. There were also survivors' stories, ranging from the incredible to the trivial. One may still marvel at the foresight of an excursionist who had provided himself both with a cap and a hat, the latter of the tall variety then in fashion. When the train stopped in the tunnel and passengers began making nervous comments at being stranded in the dark, some instinct of approaching disaster told him to remove his cap and place his hat upon his head. The crash came the next moment and he was flung violently across the compartment, but escaped with a shaking. The hat was telescoped but absorbed the shock.

3. The Steam Years – Named Trains and Cross-Countries

Two trains on the Brighton line were celebrated far outside the area it served. They were the 'City Limited' and the 'Southern Belle.' The 'City Limited' had the longer history, although not so named until 1907, and it was very much Brighton's train in that it soon became patronised by Brighton residents who lived on the coast but had their offices in London. At first, at least, the 'Southern Belle' was a luxury service for the visitor, although in the later years of the electric Belles the Pullmans regularly carried Brighton notables of the entertainment world whose work took them to London.

The antecedents of the 'City Limited' have been seen already in Chapter 2 in the 8.45am up first class train and its complementary return service in the evening. After the opening of Victoria station the train served that terminus as well at various periods either by a portion detached at Croydon or by slipping. For some 30 years the Brighton-London Bridge timings varied between 65min (achieved by the down train in 1883) and 80min. The first 60min schedule came in 1912 but by the down train only. There were slowings in World War 1, but when the service returned to normal on 21 February 1921 the up journey time was cut to 62min. Up and down journeys were both done in 60min as from 9 July 1928, by which time the LBSC was part of the Southern Railway. There was an unusual interlude from 2 September 1867 to the end of 1868 when the train ran to and from Cannon Street, calling at the South Eastern side of London Bridge (the Brighton station here is a terminus). The step was taken in an atmosphere of expectancy that the Brighton and South Eastern companies might amalgamate, but this was not to be.

Pullman Cars appeared in the train from 1875, when the rest of the coaches were still 6-wheelers. On several occasions during its life the train was favoured with rolling stock distinctly superior to the LBSC average. Bogie firsts designed by William Stroudley, and completed after his death, displaced the 6-wheelers in 1889. By 1901 the train was one of the heaviest regular expresses in the country. It then comprised 12 bogie vehicles and three 6-wheel brakes, weighing 306 tons and marshalled as follows from the engine end: 6-wheel brake, three bogie firsts, three 8-wheel Pullmans, three bogie firsts, 6-wheel brake; and a slip portion for Victoria comprising a 6-wheel brake, bogie first, 12-wheel Pullman, and bogie first. Two extra firsts were added on Mondays. In 1903 this set was painted in the livery of umber lower panels and cream above which was later adopted as standard for LBSC main line stock.

In 1907, its first year as a named train, the 'City Limited' was again favoured with new stock, this time a roomy 9ft wide overall to the designs of Earle Marsh. The formation was cut to nine vehicles, comprising: brake first and two lavatory firsts (all vestibuled together), three 8-wheel Pullmans, and the Victoria slip portion of slip brake, 12-wheel Pullman and lavatory first. The 3-car vestibuled set was an innovation for the LBSC in rationalising access to toilet compartments. Such things were provided in the previous firsts introduced by R. J. Billinton, but on a limited scale and not always easy to get at. The normal weight of the train was 304 tons but an extra first on Mondays brought it up to 330 tons.

Important changes took place in 1919 when the Victoria portion was run as a separate train and the 'City Limited' proper began taking third class passengers. Third class compartments were built into the luggage space of the brake first, third class coaches were added, and the number of Pullmans was reduced to two. The normal formation was now 10 coaches.

Acworth was much impressed by the volume of season ticket traffic from Brighton and by the amenities of the 8.45am up, commenting with particular pleasure on the fact that because the train in those days was almost a male preserve, smoking was allowed throughout the journey in the 'breakfast car' going up, and again coming home when the 'breakfast car' became a 'tea car' (he was referring to the service of meals in the Pullmans). He wrote:

'If on a given day all the season-ticket holders in Great Britain were confined to their houses for a space of four-and-twenty hours, the fact would make little difference to the appearance of the "Dutchman", or the "Flying Scotchman" (sic), or the other great expresses . . . But the best trains of the Brighton Company would be little better than strings of empty coaches. Let anyone travel by, for example, the 8.45am from Brighton, or the return train at 5pm, and notice the look of pleased surprise with which the ticket collectors accept the tender of an ordinary ticket, and he will appreciate the dimensions to which the Brighton season ticket traffic has already grown.'

The above was written in 1888 and it was noted that over the previous 13 years season ticket receipts had grown from £129,000 to £189,000. By 1899, when Acworth published a second edition, they were £235,000.

Like the 'City Limited,' the 'Southern Belle' had its

Right: **Cabs await the call from 'Something in the City' in Terminus Road, Brighton, about 1903.** *National Railway Museum, Crown Copyright*

Below: **Class B4 No 67, with extended smokebox, heads a down City express near Purley.** *Bucknall Collection/IAL*

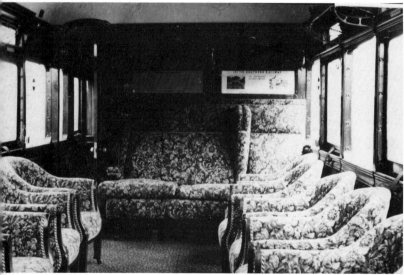

Above: 'H1' class Atlantic No 38 leaves Brighton for London Bridge. The leading vehicles are first class coaches converted for the 'City Limited' from ex-LSWR electric trailers. *H. Gordon Tidey/IAL*

Left: Saloon coach interior, the 'City Limited'. *Madgwick Collection/IAL*

Below: Class L 4-6-4T No 333, *Remembrance,* the LBSC War Memorial engine, passes Merstham with the down 'City Limited'.

origins before the name was bestowed. Pullman Cars were included in certain London-Brighton trains from 1875. In October 1881 a Pullman was fitted with electric lighting supplied from a battery of secondary cells and on 14 October made a demonstration run to Brighton with press representatives. On the down journey the lamps were switched on for short periods while passing through tunnels, but on the return trip the correspondent of *The Times* noted that they were left on throughout the journey, while the man from the *Daily Telegraph* enthused over the fact that 'all that was needed was to move the little switch, and instantaneously the delicate carbon thread enclosed in the lamps was aglow with pure white light.' Three more cars were equipped similarly and in December 1881 the four electrically-lit Pullmans provided the first all-Pullman service between London and Brighton. After a hesitant start, the service became popular and in 1882 began a schedule of two trips daily in each direction, one down journey being non-stop in

75min. This began the era of 'Pullman Limiteds' on the London-Brighton line.

The batteries of the original cars had to be charged overnight at Victoria. In 1888 a new set of cars was introduced in which the batteries were charged en route by axle-driven generators. The vehicles were also the first Pullmans in Britain to have vestibule connections so that passengers could walk from end to end of the train.

In *Our Railways* (1894) John Pendleton quotes the representative of the *Daily News* who seems to have ridden in the train on a trip for the press when it was considerably shorter than its normal composition. He wrote:

'The carriages are constructed on what is known as the "vestibule" system, the three waggons of which the train is composed having covered passageways between them. They are fitted with bay windows, and the interiors are finished in a style of unusual splendour. Mirrors are all

Above: **An early 'Pullman Limited' approaches Preston Park on the down journey. The American style Pullmans with clerestory roofs are headed by a 'B1' ('Gladstone') 0-4-2.** *Bucknall Collection/IAL*

Right: **The locomotive in this view of a down 'Pullman Limited' near Preston Park is R. J. Billinton's 4-4-0 No 213, *Bessemer*, a 'B2' with a larger boiler which was classified 'B3'. No more of the class were built.** *Bucknall Collection/IAL*

Above: **The 'Southern Belle' at Tooting Bec Common in the charge of Marsh '13' 4-4-2T No 23.** *Wentworth S. Gray/J. H. Price collection*

Left: **Atlantic No 426 was the last of the second series built by Marsh and classified 'H2'. It is illustrated heading the 'Southern Belle' about 1920.** *IAL*

Below: **The 'Southern Belle' in the Baltic tank era. Class L 4-6-4T No 332 is on the last lap of the down run at Patcham.** *Bucknall Collection/IAL*

Above right: **Brighton's gantry signals beckon the 'Belle' into the station as Class L 4-6-4T No 328 coasts home. Montpelier Junction signalbox is behind the train in the background.** *A. B. MacLeod*

around; the chairs are upholstered in old gold velvet; the windows are draped with crushed strawberry damask; the floors are covered with Wilton carpets; and the electric light is everywhere.'

Although one of the 'Pullman Limiteds' had run non-stop to Brighton, none made the journey in the hour and other trains in the same service called at Preston Park, East Croydon, or Clapham Junction in one direction or the other. It was an innovation, therefore, when on 2 October 1898 an all-Pullman train was put on on Sundays which ran non-stop in both directions with a 60min timing each way, the quickest scheduled up to that time. In 1899 the train was named the 'Brighton Limited.' It was the direct ancestor of the 'Southern Belle.'

Before this new star appeared on the LBSC stage an important improvement was made to the London-Brighton main line. Two extra tracks were completed from South Croydon to Coulsdon in 1899, and in April 1900 the quadrupling was extended by the opening of the Quarry line from Coulsdon to Earlswood, by-passing Redhill. The Quarry line was on a new location but closely parallel to the old route. Motorists today taking the link road from the top of Reigate Hill to the M23 Brighton Motorway are reminded of how close together the two lines often are by-passing under two adjacent bridges carrying the two double-tracks. The value of the Quarry line to a fast and reliable London-Brighton service was out of proportion to its modest length of 6¾ miles, for it kept trains not calling at Redhill clear of the congested section carrying traffic of the LBSC and the South Eastern.

In these propitious circumstances a daily 60min London-Brighton non-stop service in each direction, formed entirely of new first class Pullman cars, was launched on 1 November 1908. It was named the 'Southern Belle'. From 1 June 1909 it made two trips each way daily. Previous Pullmans on the Brighton line had retained an echo of their American ancestry in their clerestory roofs. In the seven new cars for the 'Belle' this

feature disappeared and the contours of the cars were closer to those becoming general for British main line stock. Advertising men in those days did not have to look nervously over their shoulders at an Advertising Standards Authority before coining a phrase and so the 'Belle' was boldly hailed as 'the most luxurious train in the world.' Movable armchairs and elegant furnishings created the impression of drawing rooms on wheels. The decor was designed with a special eye to the ladies, no doubt in recognition of their capacity for charming first class fares and Pullman supplements out of their escorts' pockets. 'A chain of vestibuled luxury' the publicity brochure called it, dwelling lovingly on the mahogany panelling inlaid with satinwood, the delicate mouldings and fluted pillars, soft green carpeting with a fleur de lys pattern, damask silk blinds and 'cosy chairs and settees in a restful shade of green morocco.' The eulogy continued: 'A woman's eyes are quick to note these things, and a woman's voice is quick to express delight. "How perfectly lovely! It is as cosy as our drawing room, Dick!"' Six of the cars were, in fact, described as 'drawing room cars'.

But the men were not neglected. Surely those two in the picture showing the amenities of the bar (decorously called the buffet) are our old friends Sherlock Holmes and Doctor Watson relaxing after one of the adventures the Doctor never got round to writing up – the Mystery of Patcham Old Place, perhaps.

Eastward and westward from Brighton along the coast lines no trains aspired to such a glamorous image. The track layout in Brighton station did not make through working easy and only one platform, Platform 3, had direct access to the main line and both coastal routes. Fig 3 shows the situation in 1911. East and west coastal services were therefore operated independently with few exceptions and passengers from one to the other had a considerable trek across the station concourse, weaving their way en route through the crowds arriving from London or waiting to join London trains. While the London-Portsmouth service was routed via Brighton

there was some smart running on the west coast section, the best train when the service began in 1848 being allowed 1hr 20min from Brighton to Portsmouth with stops at Chichester and Worthing only.

In mid-century the best time had extended to 1hr 25min, but with more stops. Two Portsmouth-Brighton trains had this timing, calling at Havant, Chichester, Woodgate for Bognor, Arundel & Littlehampton, and Worthing. Note the composite station names. The Littlehampton and Bognor branches were not yet open. Years later the west coast line saw the launch of a through service that was to keep main line steam at Brighton for years after electrification. The LBSC timetable for the summer of 1912 announced a 'Coast Line Express' between Brighton, Bournemouth, and Salisbury, with a Plymouth through coach in the Salisbury portion. The service came off during World War 1, but on the eve of Grouping, in 1922, the LBSCR, LSWR and GWR collaborated in a revival and an extension of this facility. A train left Brighton in summer at 11am with coaches for Cardiff, Ilfracombe and Bournemouth. Calling at Worthing and Chichester, it ran into Portsmouth and there divided. One portion left for Salisbury, splitting there again into a section for Westbury, Trowbridge, Bath, Bristol, Newport and Cardiff; and another for Exeter, Barnstaple Junction and Ilfracombe. The rest of the train continued from Portsmouth to Southampton and Bournemouth. A correspondent on a press trip in the eastbound direction noted that the train consisted of two LBSC coaches from Bournemouth, two LSWR from Ilfracombe, and four GWR, including a luncheon car, from Cardiff. The trip concluded with a dinner in Brighton Pavilion where the Mayor of Brighton congratulated the railway on 'putting in force a service of trains to reach the Queen of Watering Places from the West much quicker than could be done via London, with

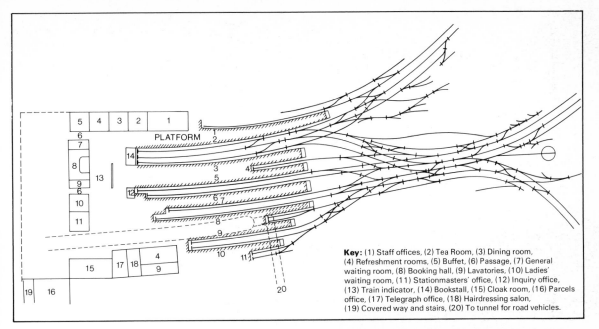

Key: (1) Staff offices, (2) Tea Room, (3) Dining room, (4) Refreshment rooms, (5) Buffet, (6) Passage, (7) General waiting room, (8) Booking hall, (9) Lavatories, (10) Ladies' waiting room, (11) Stationmasters' office, (12) Inquiry office, (13) Train indicator, (14) Bookstall, (15) Cloak room, (16) Parcels office, (17) Telegraph office, (18) Hairdressing salon, (19) Covered way and stairs, (20) To tunnel for road vehicles.

Fig 3. Brighton station in 1911 at the height of the steam era.

Right: **An all-wooden signalbox at Shoreham.** *J. Scrace*

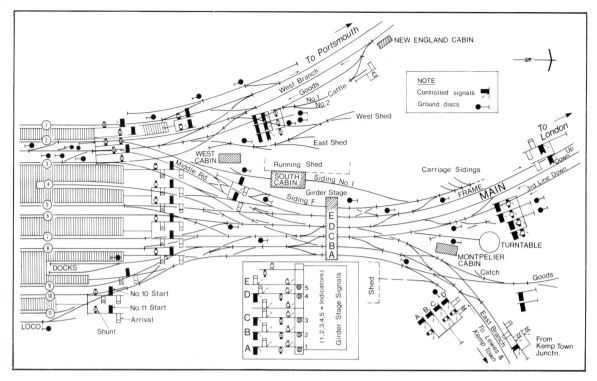

the additional advantage of no change of carriage.'

The signalling of Brighton Station at this period is shown in Fig 4.

On the east coast line in the 1850s a fast train from Hastings reached Brighton in 1hr 5min stopping only at St Leonards, Polegate and Lewes. There was a conditional stop at Bexhill to pick up passengers for Brighton and London only. It appears that this was a through train to London, the difference of only 5min between the scheduled Brighton arrival and departure times being very tight for a connection. A similar service was advertised from London to Hastings via Brighton with a Brighton-Hastings time of 1hr 20min. Until 1912 passengers for stations east of Hastings had to change there into a South Eastern train but in that year a through service was put on from Brighton via Hastings to Ashford, Folkestone, Dover, Walmer and Deal. There were connections at Ashford for Canterbury, Ramsgate, and Margate. These trains did not convey local passengers between Brighton and Hastings. The Brighton-Dover trains were not resumed after World War 1 but through services between Brighton and Ashford continued under the Southern Railway until the east coast line was electrified in 1937.

In spite of Brighton station's layout problems, there was some through working between the east coast and west coast lines. The summer timetable of 1912 announced a new service, the 'South Coast Express' between Hastings and Portsmouth Harbour, making the journey westbound in 2hr 32min and eastbound in 2hr 25min with stops at St Leonards, Bexhill, Eastbourne, Polegate, Lewes, Brighton, Worthing, Chichester and

Fig 4. Semaphore signalling at Brighton.

Above right: **Braypool Cutting box, south of Clayton Tunnel, is typical of the smaller main line boxes in later years.** *Bucknall Collection/IAL*

Right: **No 213,** *Bessemer,* **the only 'B3', at Balham with the 'Sunny South Special'.** *British Rail*

Havant. 'South Coast Express' appeared in the timetable columns, although this distinction was not given to the 'Coast Line Express' except in the announcement at the beginning of the book. Also in 1912 there was a slower, unnamed, through service taking 2hr 45min from Hastings to Portsmouth and 2hr 50min in the reverse direction. The 'South Coast Express' is reported to have been formed of four LSWR coaches. With this short formation and a tank locomotive it may have been possible to get in and out of Platform 3 by the east/west connection but other comments at this period suggest that shunting was usually involved in transfers between the two coastal lines.

The best known of the Brighton named trains after the 'Southern Belle' and the 'City Limited' was the 'Sunny South Special'. It was inaugurated in 1905 as a development of a through carriage service between Manchester, Liverpool and Brighton which had been introduced a year earlier. A joint venture with the LNWR, it was formed of that company's stock with restaurant car. Portions from Manchester and Liverpool combined at Crewe, coaches from Birmingham were picked up at

Above: **A 'B4' leaving Brighton with the 'Sunny South Special' gives the train the Billinton look.** *Bucknall Collection/IAL*

Above right: **The exploits of Marsh 'I3' tanks when running through between Brighton and Willesden with the 'Sunny South Special' are a celebrated episode in LBSC history. No 21 of the class heads the train at Balham.** *IAL*

Right: **Paddington to Brighton in 1905. 'B4' No 52,** *Siemens,* **pauses with the through train at Addison Road, Kensington (the present Kensington Olympia).** *L. E. Brailsford/IAL*

Rugby, and the train ran through to Eastbourne via Brighton. The route through outer London was from Willesden Junction to Clapham Junction via Addison Road (now Kensington Olympia). LBSC engines normally worked to and from Willesden Junction but in 1909 occurred the celebrated through working of 'I3' class superheated 4-4-2Ts Nos 23 and 26 between Brighton and Rugby which opened LNWR eyes to the merits of superheating. The 'I3s' worked both ways on one bunker full of coal and did not take water between East Croydon and Rugby. Willesden to Rugby was run non-stop with the 250 ton train at an average speed of 52.6mph. Between the wars the train was extended to Hastings, still running via Brighton. Although it did not reappear under its old name after World War 2, the 'Sunny South' was the forerunner of several through services between the North, the Midlands and Sussex that took the Willesden Junction-Clapham Junction route up to the early 1960s.

The same cross-London link was used for a short time between Clapham Junction and Addison Road by a through LBSC service between Brighton and Paddington intended to save passengers for GWR destinations the trouble of crossing London from Victoria or London Bridge. Beginning on 2 July 1906, the up train left Brighton at 11.30am and with stops at East Croydon, Clapham Junction, and Addison Road reached Paddington at 1.10pm. The route from Addison Road to

Paddington was via Uxbridge Road junction and the Hammersmith & City line to Westbourne Park. Returning from Paddington at 3.40pm, the train made the same stops and reached Brighton at 5.17pm. The normal formation was five non-corridor coaches. After a year the train was withdrawn for lack of support.

If the Paddington venture was a failure, Brightonians in the know would often use the 'Sunny South' train for journeys to London, reaching their destinations by bus from Addison Road or, in later years, by Bakerloo tube from Willesden. The attraction was the superb ride in the 12-wheel LNWR restaurant car, better than anything the ordinary LBSC coaches could provide, and accompanied by a full luncheon service for half-a-crown (12½p) or

Left: Birkenhead-Hastings (via Brighton) through coaches cross the River Ouse at Lewes behind 'I3' 4-4-2T No 32078 on 13 August 1949.
S. C. Nash

Below left: An unidentified 'Schools' 4-4-0 leaves Brighton with the through train to Cardiff in the summer of 1946.
Author

Right: 'H2' class Atlantic No 32424, *Beachy Head,* approaches Addison Road with a through service from the London Midland Region to Brighton, Eastbourne and Hastings on 5 August 1950. *IAL*

Below: A Leicester-Hastings train with 4-4-2 No 32424 at the head passes South Croydon. *C. Hogg*

Above left: **Southern Region 'U1' class 2-6-0 No 31901 heads a High-Wycombe-Littlehampton excursion (via Preston Park and the Cliftonville curve to Hove) near Clayton Tunnel on 18 April 1954.** *S. C. Nash*

Left: **British Rail standard steam comes to Brighton – Class 4 2-6-0 No 76059 passes Patcham with a Leicester-Hastings through train on 2 July 1955.** *W. M. J. Jackson*

Above: **After diesels had taken over from steam on Brighton line inter-Regional workings, Class 33 No D6558 nears Three Bridges with a Wolverhampton-Brighton excursion.** *J. Scrace*

three shillings and sixpence (17½p) if one really meant to push the boat out.

From Grouping to World War 2 a service from Birkenhead and Birmingham to Hastings via Reading and Redhill was routed through Brighton. This was a portion of a long-established through train between Birkenhead and the Kent Coast which continued from Redhill to Tonbridge and the South Eastern main line. Up to Grouping its Hastings coaches had been detached at Tonbridge. After the switch to the LBSC route via Brighton the Birkenhead-Hastings service ran as a separate train in summer and there was an additional Birmingham (Snow Hill)-Brighton-Hastings service on

summer Saturdays. These trains were restored after World War 2. In the spring of 1962 the through coaches did not go beyond Eastbourne and they were withdrawn in the autumn. They returned briefly in 1964 but the northern limit of their journey was now Wolverhampton. At the beginning of September they were withdrawn.

The longest-lived of the cross-country trains serving Brighton were those to the west. In later years they were expanded into three separate trains from Brighton to Bournemouth, to Cardiff, and to Plymouth. They are remembered for the sight of Bulleid's light Pacifics, both 'air-smoothed' and rebuilt relieving the monotony of emus on the west coast line from Brighton after World War 2. Pacifics were stationed at Brighton for these workings but they also brought a considerable variety of steam motive power including 'Schools', 'U1' class 2-6-0s and the second series of Brighton Atlantics. Only the Plymouth train survived the Beeching cuts, but was curtailed to Exeter. From 1963 Class 33 diesels began to alternate with the light Pacifics as steam allocations to Brighton were reduced. For a short time early in 1964 the train was diverted into Fratton so that the Bulleid Co-Co electric locomotives could be used between there and Brighton. There was a brief return of steam working in 1966 but a twilight period was setting in which saw the Brighton-Exeter service reduced to Saturdays only and later operated by spare Hastings diesel 6-car sets. Traffic picked up, however, and from 7 May 1977 an 8-coach train including a buffet car, hauled by a Class 33, was substituted.

Left: Regular through trains between the London Midland Region and the Sussex Coast have been supplemented by excursions for many years. Here Stanier 'Black Five' No 45416 leaves Clayton Tunnel with a Nuneaton-Brighton special on 6 August 1961. *S. Creer*

Below: A spare Hastings diesel set forms a Brighton-Exeter service. *G. F. Gillham*

4. Brighton Works and Locomotives

The locomotives in the pool from which the Brighton line drew its motive power in the early days were maintained and repaired at New Cross in South London. Conditions here were congested, and both the London & Brighton and the South Eastern Railway relieved the pressure by building repair shops of their own. By the time the pooled locomotives were distributed to the individual companies in 1846, Brighton already had several engineering shops adjacent to the station which undertook repairs to locomotives and stationary engines, and various metalwork. Carriage and wagon work was dispersed among several places on the system, including Brighton, where the shops were on the opposite side of the line to the other engineering establishment, which was on the eastern side and formed the nucleus of Brighton Works. Locomotive building did not begin there until the early 1850s. The print of the Brighton railway viaduct on page 13, published in 1846, shows the workshops and a chimney on the east of the line as it approaches the terminus.

With the coming of the railway the population of Brighton increased dramatically and acquired an industrial element. From 1831 to 1841 only 437 new houses were built in the town. In the next 10 years the number swelled to 2,806. Where once there had been only half a dozen straggling streets on the slopes below the station there were soon 50 'closely lined with houses and thickly inhabited by a thriving and industrious population, a large proportion of whom, probably, derive their subsistence from the railway.' To meet the needs of industrial workers in a town where previously employment had been mainly in fishing and agriculture, a Mechanics' Institute was established on 23 October 1848. It was a period of social unrest across the Channel, but here, said a correspondent in the *Brighton Herald,* the visitor would see 'in all probability a thousand earnest men – working men met without political excitement of any kind, but with high and stern determination', and he found this peaceful zeal for self-improvement 'in singular contrast with the physical revolutions of continental society'.

At first the housing for the 'thriving and industrious population' was far from satisfactory. There were problems of ventilation and drainage in the thickly clustered dwellings, and in the same year that the Mechanics' Institute was founded a certain Dr Kebble wrote that 'no-one accustomed to fresh air can walk through the streets without being nauseated by the smells.' These problems receded from 1870 onwards with improvements in water supply and sewage disposal, and demolition of old buildings.

There were, of course, undesirables among the worthies, and when in 1844 a former Superintendent of the London & Brighton Railway Police applied for the post of Chief Constable of Brighton he was recommended for his knowledge of the 'improper characters' in the habit of visiting the town and residing in it.

Brighton Works as a centre of locomotive building were the creation of John Chester Craven, a figure who seems to have been cast in the sternest Victorian mould. When he joined the LBSCR in 1847 as Locomotive Superintendent he had already had experience of moving the Eastern Counties Railway's works from Romford to Stratford. It fell to him to expand the repair shops on their somewhat restricted site adjacent to Brighton passenger station. Horley was considered briefly as a site for a new works but it was decided to augment what already existed at Brighton.

Brighton is a town of diverse aspects. One talks of 'cultural Brighton' and 'candyfloss Brighton'. The 1850s saw the development of 'railway Brighton' around the station and works. Eric Gill, the sculptor and typographer, who lived as a boy in the 1880s in the Prestonville Road, wrote in his autobiography of 'a railway with a sort of nondescript encampment crowding round it ... a congeries of more or less sordid streets growing like a fungus wherever the network of railways and sidings and railway sheds would allow.' Another Brighton notable who knew this part of the town was Magnus Volk, the pioneer of electric passenger transport in Great Britain. His son Conrad has related in his biography of his father that in the late 1850s the young Magnus was often to be seen in Prestonville Road where it crosses the west coast line, watching the trains emerging from the tunnel beneath his feet and curving towards the station. Perhaps memories of these early spotting excursions turned the inventive young man's thoughts in later years towards the improvement of railway traction.

The works were on the east side of the main line immediately north of the passenger station and overlooking the valley through which the London road entered the town. The slopes of the valley to the east of the site and the station buildings to the south limited expansion in those directions, while extension to the north was restricted by the line to Lewes swinging eastwards towards its viaduct. Originally the locomotive depot was on the same site.

Above and above right: **Brighton Works from the west in the 1870s.** *Madgwick Collection/IAL*

Right: **Craven's works at Brighton are seen beyond the chalk hill in this early photograph taken from above the tunnel on the west coast line where once Magnus Volk watched trains. Removal of the chalk is in progress in order to make room for the locomotive depot, which at this time was on the works site.** *Madgwick Collection/IAL*

Power for the machinery in the works was provided at first by an old Sharp single, No 25, which was stripped of its driving wheels and fitted up for a belt drive to the shafting. It was later replaced by a vertical steam engine. The works had their own well, 170ft deep, for water supply, from which water was pumped to an overhead tank by a compound beam engine which had once driven pumps for the atmospheric system of the London & Croydon Railway. There was no foundry at first, castings being bought from outside.

In 1852 the works produced their first home-built locomotives – two small single-driver well tanks. These were the first of a great variety of locomotives built under the Craven regime. Each class was small in numbers and needed its own spare parts, leading to chronic congestion in the works. Some 40 years later Acworth commented on the 'extraordinary variety' of the Brighton engines, which he thought arose largely from 'the conscientious desire of an earlier generation of engineers to prove all things, coupled perhaps with some slight neglect of the second clause of the Apostolic precept enjoining us to "hold fast to that which is good".' When William Stroudley took over from Craven in 1870 the LBSCR is said to have had 72 different classes of engine in use. Presumably this number included locomotives bought from outside in the early years and modified in various ways to suit Craven's ideas and requirements.

Brighton residents were dramatically reminded of the railway industry in their midst on 17 March 1853 when 'a loud report resembling the explosion of a large cannon' startled Mr Craven as he was about to begin shaving. It came from the station, and witnesses reported that 'a mass of smoke and vapour enveloped everything, but as this cleared off it was seen that a large portion of the westernmost shed was blown off, and upon the remaining portions were the fragments of an engine.' These were the remains of a tank engine, No 10, whose boiler had blown up shortly before it was due to depart with an early morning train for Littlehampton. No 10, said to have been cut down from a larger engine, had recently been through the works, and with the driver and fireman on this occasion was a fitter who was to watch its performance. All three were killed. An official statement quickly issued by the LBSCR said that the Directors 'had too much cause to believe that the accident arose from the driver having screwed down the safety valves shortly before the accident took place.'

An inquest was held, and Craven was closely questioned by the jury over supervision in the works. No connection could be established between the work which had just been carried out on No 10 and the cause of the explosion but the jury was clearly uneasy about the number of changes that had been made since the engine was new in 1840. In a phrase giving a glimpse of his methods, Craven explained that 'engines are like an Irishman's coat; they are patched and patched till they are nearly re-built.'

Evidently the safety valves had been in order to start

with. The assistant stationmaster had 'observed that the driver was standing up on the hand railing by the side of the boiler warming his coffee at the top of the safety valve, the steam from which was blowing off'. Craven was further questioned about his encouragement to enginemen to save steam, which might have led them to tamper with the valve settings, but this line of inquiry proved inconclusive. On the other hand evidence from other railwaymen did show that the driver of No 10 that day had made adjustments. The inquest was adjourned after 6½ hours. When it was resumed the next day the jury's verdict was 'that the death of the driver, John Young, was caused by his own reckless conduct in placing a higher pressure on the engine than it was fitted to bear'. He was also found guilty of manslaughter in causing the deaths of his two colleagues on the footplate. All members of the jury concurred in a recommendation that 'in future a more frequent and rigid examination be made of the locomotive engines'. It is difficult to escape a feeling that Craven was not popular in some Brighton circles, but in others he must have been highly regarded for after his retirement he was made an alderman.

When locomotive production began at Brighton the works expanded, always in the face of severe space problems. A new wheel shop was authorised in 1854. The range of activities carried on in the restricted site was remarkable, including marine work and jobs for the Signal and Freight Departments. In 1855 two boilers were built for the steamer *Paris* belonging to the firm of Maple & Morris which operated the Newhaven-Dieppe service for the LBSCR. It is small wonder that under Craven boiler-making spilled over into the erecting shop. Further machinery was acquired in 1860 and 1861, and in the latter year a new carriage shop was built, but still detached from the main works.

In the early days of the works the locomotive and carriage sidings were on the same site. There was much shunting in the yard, and often these movements encroached on the main lines, delaying the departure of trains. Looking for more siding space, Craven decided to remove a hill of chalk which had been dumped between the main and west coast lines and came from excavations when the line was built. Brighton Council at first objected, apparently regarding the hill as serving a useful purpose in screening the railway from the eyes of local residents who might prefer the view of a chalk mountain, even if artificially erected, to the mundane sight of locomotives and carriages. Craven then revived the idea of moving the works to Horley, whereupon the Council relented, not wishing to lose an enterprise which brought considerable material benefit to the town. The chalk was removed to various sites on the system. It was a long process, lasting from 1854 until the early 1860s, and the benefit was felt not by Craven but by his successor, William Stroudley, who was able to move the locomotive depot to the cleared site, where it remained until the end of steam.

Craven retired in 1869. When Stroudley took over his job in 1870 he applied himself to reducing the variety of locomotive classes and cutting down the conglomeration

of spare parts that had been necessary to keep such a varied family of locomotives in service. His policy was to develop six standard classes with interchangeable components, so that a relatively small stock of spares would suffice to meet requirements on demand and speed the passage of locomotives through the works. Stroudley's clarity of thought expressed itself also in attention to detail. In the works he insisted on precision in machining, and he saw that it was achieved by encouraging craftsmanship in individuals and in gangs of men engaged on specialised tasks. This policy extended even to the painting of names on the engines which was in the hands of one man from Stroudley's advent until hand-painting was discontinued.

As soon as he was in office Stroudley began to make changes in the organisation of the works. He had carriage and wagon building transferred from the west side of the line to the main works site on the east, and the locomotive depot was moved to the west, taking advantage of the additional space made available by removal of the chalk hill. Craven's erecting shop was turned into a smithy and a new one was built. Then a foundry was added for the works to produce their own castings, and a new shop for Westinghouse brake parts was built. To compensate for these extra activities on the main site, the paint shop was moved to the west side of the line (Fig 5). A new coppersmiths' shop was built in 1881.

The new chief had decided views on boiler construction, believing that machine riveting so squeezed the rivets that the holes in the plates were expanded and caused cracks. His method of boiler making was to put the plates in a frame and drill the rivet holes while the plates were together so that the holes would be dead true. The plates were then taken out of the frame and the boiler was built by hand riveting them together. Steam joints were made true and a little boiled oil applied.

In 1880 it was decided that the works should be relieved of their marine repairs and this activity was moved to new workshops at Newhaven, although it still remained under Stroudley's control. His fame rests on more solid foundations than the yellow ochre locomotive livery (officially 'Stroudley's improved engine green') he introduced and the immaculate condition in which it was kept, or the practice of naming all his engines, but these are the things which have come first to the mind of generations of enthusiasts. He should be remembered also for having brought classical order and harmony to the Gothic wilderness of the old Brighton Works as Craven had left them.

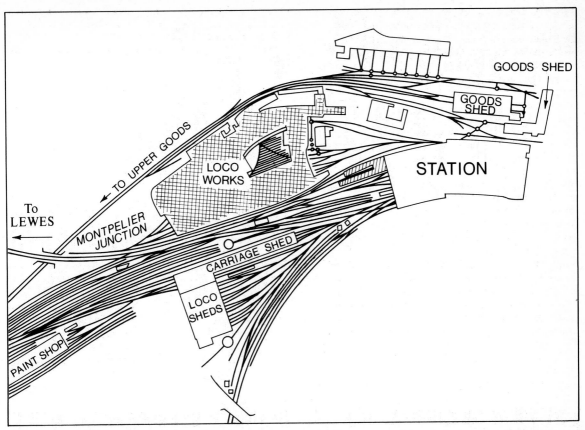

Top: **Machinery driven by belts from overhead shafting.** *Madgwick Collection/IAL*

Above: **This view of Brighton Works from the east taken in 1959 shows in the left foreground the extension built out over the line to the Lower Yard (goods) by R. J. Billinton. The goods line is on the embankment beyond the roof tops in the foreground and crosses the New England Road on the single-arch bridge seen in the centre of the picture.** *IAL*

Left: **The erecting shop.** *Madgwick Collection/IAL*

Above right: **Class H2 Atlantic No 32421, *South Foreland,* under heavy repair in Brighton Works.** *Brian Morrison*

Stroudley died in 1889 and was succeeded by R. J. Billinton. The LBSC locomotive stock was now expanding rapidly and during Billinton's regime it increased from 410 in 1890 to 535 by 1902. The new CME carried on Stroudley's standardisation and spares policy, and also began the practice of storing spare boilers. He provided more space in the works by building out over the goods lines on the eastern side, supporting the new floor space on brick piles. The extension was 430ft long and from 41 to 53ft wide. This was the cylinder shop, iron store and spring shop. Even so, congestion remained a problem and Billinton's 0-6-0 goods engines, although a product of the Brighton drawing office, were built outside by the Vulcan Foundry, the class being known as 'the Vulcans' in consequence.

A visitor to Brighton Works in Billinton's day wrote an account of them in the Sussex magazine *Views and Reviews* in July 1896. At that time the LBSC Locomotive Department had a staff of about 3,850, of whom 2,200 (including drivers and firemen) were stationed at Brighton. At the same period the Pullman Car Company

was assembling its cars in Brighton Works from parts sent over from America. It had moved to Brighton from Derby after its contract to build cars for the Midland Railway expired in 1881. In later years the building of Pullman Cars was taken over by contractors, but the Pullman company continued to maintain the vehicles itself. A building on the up side of the line just south of Preston Park, which had been used by the LBSC for locomotive maintenance, was vacated in 1928 and Pullman repair and renovation activities were transferred to it. These works were closed in 1963 under the Beeching rationalisation measures and Pullman maintenance was transferred to other railway works. The vacant building was used for some time for storing preserved steam locomotives, which from time to time were put on display at railway open days at Brighton station.

In 1896 Brighton Works were building 12 locomotives a year and there were always 40 or 50 going through the shops for maintenance and repairs. By this time electric power was being used for some purposes and the works had its own generating plant consisting of 'three large dynamos and three beautiful steam engines.' A fourth stationary engine drove the plant in the nearby sawmill. The foundry was in full swing and comprised two cupolas 'supplied with a powerful blast from a Roots Patent Blower.' In the smithy seven steam hammers were installed, two of 30cwt and the others of 8, 10 or 15cwt. The wheel turnery was equipped with an hydraulic press capable of exerting a force of some 400 tons. Of his impressions in the fitting and turning shop the visitor wrote: 'It seems as if every tool and appliance ever invented for cutting, planing, turning, drilling, twisting, bending or in any way manipulating metal were here congregated together.'

The erecting shop had been almost doubled in length in 1892. Two tracks extended from end to end. Some work at this period was being carried out in buildings on the opposite side of the main line as had been the practice in Craven's day. The activities noted in this detached area were the upholstery works, the cart and van building department, a shed for minor repairs, and the wagon and goods brake building shed. In Billinton's day consideration was given to moving the carriage and

wagon work away from Brighton and a survey of possible sites was begun in 1896. Eventually land was bought at Lancing, between Shoreham and Worthing, and building began, but the new carriage & wagon works was not fully operational until 1912.

Under D. Earle Marsh, who succeeded Billinton in 1905, some internal reorganisation took place, carriage and wagon underframes being built in separate shops pending completion of the new rolling stock works at Lancing. When this establishment was ready the wagon shop at Brighton was handed over to the Locomotive Department for running repairs. A new storey was added to the works building by raising the roof over the wheel and Westinghouse shops by 13ft. In 1908 the works were connected to the Brighton electricity supply, all machinery was converted to electric drive, and the steam-driven generating plant was scrapped. A steam heating plant was installed in the paint shop in the same year.

The last Locomotive Superintendent of the LBSC was L. B. Billinton (son of R. J.) who took office in 1911. The works were then approaching their zenith as a locomotive

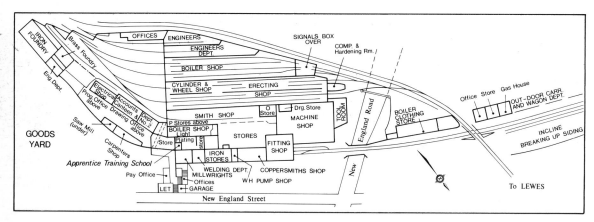

Fig 6. Brighton Works in 1945.

Left: 'H1' Atlantic No 2039, *Hartland Point,* after modification to test the sleeve valve gear developed for the 'Leader' project. *IAL*

Right: The first 'Leader' class locomotive is lowered on to its bogies in Brighton Works. *National Railway Museum Crown Copyright*

building establishment and moving into a 'big engine' era. The main block was then over 600ft long and nearly 450ft wide at the maximum; it narrowed towards the 'country' end where the site was bounded by the New England Road. Principal areas inside the building were the boiler shop, 505ft long and for about half its length 126ft wide; the erecting shop, 593ft long and 98ft wide, and the machine shop, 207ft long and 140ft wide, in five bays. Alongside the erecting shop and extending 334ft was the forge, 54ft wide and opening into the smithy, with the frame shop and wheel shop adjoining. A separate group of buildings beyond the New England Road included the coppersmiths' shop. Billinton was responsible for a fleet of 610 locomotives.

In World War 1 Brighton Works contributed to munitions production and other wartime engineering requirements. At the end of hostilities Grouping was already in sight and with it an uncertain outlook. The last locomotive built at Brighton before the LBSCR was merged into the Southern Railway was the 4-6-4T No 333, *Remembrance*, the company's war memorial locomotive, which was completed in April 1922.

In the early Grouping years Brighton produced some locomotives for R. E. L. Maunsell, the Southern's first CME. Ten of the 'River' class 2-6-4 tanks were built at the works in 1926, followed in 1928 by 10 'U' class 2-6-0s. In 1929 the works turned out the eight powerful 'Z' class 0-8-0 tanks. Thereafter most of the work which had been done at Brighton was transferred to Ashford and Eastleigh, together with almost all the machinery, although the works continued to carry out running repairs on locomotives, coaches, and eventually electric multiple-unit stock.

But productive activity was to return to Brighton Works. In 1942 it was again on war work, having been almost completely re-equipped. Towards the end of World War 2 the works undertook some operations on Bulleid light Pacifics and 104 were erected there. The thousandth engine to emerge new from Brighton was the light Pacific No 34064, *Battle of Britain*. Fig 6 shows the extent of the works in 1945.

On the eve of nationalisation the works converted Atlantic No 32039, *Hartland Point*, for testing the sleeve valve gear developed by O. V. S. Bulleid for his 'Leader'

Left: **A first and probably surreptitious glimpse of the 'Leader' outside the Works.** *H. M. Madgwick*

Centre left: **The 'Leader' passes Lewes, running bunker-end first, on a trial run from Brighton to Crowborough.** *C. C. B. Herbert*

Bottom left: **'Terrier' No 3775 (formerly No 635) in Stroudley livery as Brighton Works shunter in 1947.** *O. J. Morris*

Below: **Craven 2-2-2 No 153 built at Brighton in 1854. After rebuilding by Stroudley it was named** *Spithead* **and numbered 164.** *IAL*

class power-bogie steam tank locomotive. Its appearance sadly marred by rebuilding, No 32039 ran trials between Brighton and St Leonards or Groombridge. Meanwhile the first 'Leader' was being built at Brighton Works in conditions of exaggerated secrecy characteristic of steam chief mechanical engineers when they attempted something out of the ordinary. A snapshot obtained by stealth published in *The Railway Gazette* was the first indication most people had of its appearance. The first and only 'Leader' to be completed went untimely to the scrap heap.

The guinea pig Atlantic made a brief appearance in passenger service with the three Hastings-Birkenhead through coaches in 1949, working them between Brighton and Redhill. After a failure of the Atlantic at Earlswood the duty was given back to more conventional power. But Brighton did move successfully into the new railway age by building the Southern's 1Co-Co1 diesel-electric No 10203, which was turned out from the works in 1953.

Visitors to Brighton at this period sometimes rubbed their eyes at seeing a 'Brighton yellow' engine outside the works. This was the 'Terrier' used as works shunter. Last of the line was No 2635, transferred from the Hayling Island branch. In its new role it was repainted in Stroudley livery, lettered *Brighton Works*, and given the number 377S.

In their centenary year, 1952, Brighton Works covered nine acres and employed a staff of about 650. The boiler shop was then in two bays, each served by two electric cranes of 30 tons and 20 tons capacity. At the south end a 30ton electric crane spanned both bays and was used for lifting boilers for riveting in a 90ton riveting machine powered by a self-contained hydraulic system. Other equipment in the shop comprised plate levelling rolls, a plate edge planer for preparation of plates before welding, a battery of radial drilling machines, and a 250 ton flanging press served by a creosote/pitch fired furnace. Portable grinding and milling machines were operated by compressed air. A high-frequency (400Hz) electrical supply was provided for the drives of high-speed machines used in drilling and tapping fireboxes.

The erecting shop was also in two bays. Locomotive repairs were concentrated in the west bay, served by overhead travelling cranes of 40 tons, 35 tons and 25 tons capacity. The east bay, largely devoted to building new locomotives, was served by two 35ton overhead travelling cranes.

Equipment in the machine shop comprised lathes, drilling, planing, grinding and milling machines, mostly with individual motor drives. There were also fitting, coppersmiths', and piping shops, and a small brass foundry. Compressed air for the works was supplied by three compressors with a combined delivery of

approximately 1,200cu ft/min. An hydraulic plant supplied water at 1,500lb/sq in.

In these post-nationalisation years the works designed some of the BR Standard steam locomotives, including '9F' 2-10-0s. One hundred and thirty of the Class 4 Standard 2-6-4 tanks were built there, including No 80154, the last new locomotive turned out, and after its emergence on 20 March 1957 the run-down began. Locomotive repair work continued until 1958, after which some of the equipment and premises were used for a time on motorcar assembly. This was a short-term reprieve and demolition began in 1969 to clear the site for a car park.

The locomotives built at Brighton have been the subject of devoted research and study, beginning with F. Burtt in 1903. Early history of motive power on the Brighton line is complex. It is typical of the problems encountered by historians that a witness at the inquest following the boiler explosion at Brighton station in 1853 referred to the locomotive involved as *Satellite,* but other sources show the ill-fated No 10 as *Vulture.* It might have been a simple lapse of memory, but one cannot discount the possibility that locomotives ready to leave the works after repairs may sometimes have been sent out with the nameplates nearest to hand rather than the ones they came in with.

Craven built various 2-2-2 classes for main line passenger traffic, sometimes incorporating features of the 'Sharpies' and 'Jenny Linds' which had been bought from outside. The hand of his son William has been seen in some of the later designs, notably in two 7ft singles built in 1863 for working the fast first class business trains. They have been judged among the best-looking engines south of the Thames in their day. In 1862, however, Craven had adopted the 2-4-0 wheel arrangement which was to become his standard for passenger work. Some of

Above: **From 1862 Craven standardised the 2-4-0 for ordinary passenger duties. No 188 was one of a batch built to his specification by Beyer, Peacock in 1864.** *IAL*

Left: **Craven's 0-4-4 well tank No 231 built at Brighton in 1866 for the South London line.** *IAL*

Right: **No 467 was Stroudley's first engine for the LBSCR. This 0-4-2T came out in 1871 as No 21. It is seen in Horsham shed in 1887.** *Bucknall Collection/IAL*

Centre right: **After rebuilding (very drastically) some Craven singles as 2-4-0s, Stroudley produced his own version of this wheel arrangement in 1873 in two engines numbered 201 and 202. This picture shows No 202,** *Goodwood.* *Madgwick Collection/IAL*

Below: **Stroudley's first 'Terrier' 0-6-0 tank engines appeared in 1872. No 40,** *Brighton,* **belonged to a batch turned out in 1878. Put on show at the Paris Exhibition in that year, she earned a gold medal, a fact recorded on her side tanks in the picture.** *Bucknall Collection/IAL*

these engines were built at Brighton and others by outside contractors, and they exhibited a confusing variety of dimensional variations. The 2-4-0 was a popular wheel arrangement at that time, and Craven also followed contemporary practice in his inside-cylinder 0-6-0 goods engines – early examples of what was to become the classic British type for freight working. His tank engines were often 'one-off' designs produced for a particular service, and were subject during their working lives to tinkering in various ways, but his 2-4-0 tank design for the Norwood Junction-Crystal Palace-Battersea-Victoria line ran to six engines.

When Stroudley took over at Brighton he first met main line passenger needs with rebuilds of Craven singles and 2-4-0s, supplementing them with new construction to the same pattern. Developments in the London area soon found Brighton Works engaged on one of the most celebrated and longest-lived of the Stroudley classes. The first section of the East London Railway from New Cross to the north bank of the Thames at Wapping had been opened on 6 December 1869, passing under the river in the tunnel built by the Brunels for horse and pedestrian traffic. This line was worked by the LBSCR, and the Stroudley 0-6-0 Class A engines (the 'Terriers') were specifically designed for working over its steep gradients and light permanent way. They weighed only 24ton 7cwt. The first of the class of 50 appeared from Brighton Works in 1872. On 10 April 1876 the East London was extended to join the Great Eastern Railway at Bishopsgate, enabling its trains to run to and from Liverpool Street. The 'Terriers' were also ideally suited

Below: **The 'D' class 0-4-2 tanks were for main line passenger work. No 239, *Patcham,* was one of a batch built by Neilson & Co in 1881.** *IAL*

Right: **No 490 was a 2-2-2 supplied by Robert Stephenson in 1864 as No 200. It was renumbered in 1887 by Stroudley and named *Dieppe.* He had begun the practice of naming engines with No 199 of the same class, which received the name *Paris.*** *IAL*

Centre right: **Stroudley's first 0-4-2 tender engines, foreshadowing the 'Gladstones', were his Class D2. No 312, *Albion,* was built at Brighton in 1883, but the first of the class appeared in 1876.** *IAL*

Bottom right: **In 1880 Class G appeared, Stroudley's last and most numerous single drivers. They were particularly associated with the light but fast Portsmouth trains. No 329, *Stephenson,* went into traffic in 1881.** *LPC/IAL*

for smart running between numerous stops on the South London line and it was with this Victoria-London Bridge service that the class became particularly associated.

Stroudley's 0-4-2 Class D tanks, equally renowned, were less specialised in origin. The 'Terriers' had 4ft dia wheels, but the 5ft 6in dia drivers of the 'D' class made them useful passenger engines for most secondary services with the ability to work fast main line and excursion traffic when necessary, subject to opportunities to take water en route on the longer runs. The class numbered 125 engines, of which 90 were built at

Brighton and 35 by Neilson & Company. Brighton produced the first of the class in 1873.

For fast passenger traffic Stroudley designed several classes of singles, culminating in the 24 Class G 2-2-2s of 1880, of which No 329, *Stephenson*, was chosen as the insignia of the Stephenson Locomotive Society. Already, however, Stroudley had begun building 0-4-2 tender engines, his first being the 'D2' mixed traffic class of 1876 with 5ft 6in wheels. All these 14 engines except No 312, *Albion*, had 'Continental' names and were often to be seen on express parcels trains between London and Newhaven in connection with the Dieppe service. A 6ft 6in version, Class D3, followed in 1878, but Stroudley's most celebrated 0-4-2 tender engines were the 'Gladstones,' or Class B, which appeared at the end of 1882. These, too, had 6ft 6in coupled wheels but larger cylinders and more heating surface than the 'D3s'.

In later years, to irreverent northern eyes not made misty by the indefinable Brighton mystique, the 'Gladstones' had an antique look. Leading coupled wheels were unusual for a main line express class, but as J. Pearson Pattinson explained in *British Railways* (1893): 'None of the Brighton locomotives have bogies, the turntables on the system not being large enough to permit this.' Acworth in *The Railways of England* (1888) made the same comment, adding that 'longer turntables would mean in many cases – at Victoria, for instance – the purchase and demolition of adjoining property.' Both were ardent admirers of the 'Gladstones.' Pearson Pattinson said the class 'is one of the finest in England and capable of the very hardest work.' Acworth, in a characteristically racy passage, wrote:

'The 8.45am up from Brighton is probably one of the heaviest expresses in the world; on a Monday morning it sometimes starts with 26 coaches on, or say a gross load of 360 tons. To Redhill the journey is just 30 miles, and

although it begins with a dead pull away from the curved platforms up a gradient of 1 in 264, it must be accomplished to the minute, under the penalty of having to crawl behind a South Eastern stopping train all the way from Redhill to London. And be the day fine or rough, and be the rails dry or greasy, the run – 30 miles in 40 minutes – is accomplished without fail. Nor does *Gladstone*, to whose leadership the train is usually consigned, ever find it necessary to appeal to a colleague for support.'

Pearson Pattinson was more guarded, simply noting that 'one of this class (ie the "B" class) has frequently passed Redhill in 40 minutes from Brighton, with a load of over 20 coaches'. But he quoted a run with a 'Gladstone' recorded by Rous-Marten, with a gross load of 335 tons 14cwt, on which speed never fell below 39mph on the long banks at 1 in 264 and the speed generally on that gradient was over 40mph. He added, with a burst of enthusiasm, 'No engines in the kingdom could much improve on a performance like this . . .' but he joined with Acworth in regretting that Brighton timetables did not give Stroudley's engines more opportunity to show their powers.

Even in their prime the 'Gladstones' sometimes had

less prestigious duties. There is a record of one of the class shedded at Brighton which regularly appeared on the Three Bridges-East Grinstead branch, having reached Three Bridges via Steyning and Horsham. It was turned at Three Bridges shed and then worked through via East Grinstead to Tunbridge Wells. The return working to Brighton is believed to have been via Uckfield and Lewes. The observer who recorded these trips in the 1891-96 period noted that they were the only 'Gladstones' working on the East Grinstead line. All other turns between Three Bridges and East Grinstead were headed by engines of other classes shedded at Three Bridges, Horsham or Tunbridge Wells.

An interesting impression of the Brighton line in 1893, when the Stroudley image was still strong, was recorded by a visitor from the West Midlands. He was disappointed to see nothing larger than a 0-4-2 tank engine (presumably a 'D' tank) at Victoria, and wrote: 'The carriages, largely 4-wheelers and very scantily upholstered, did not at all appeal to me. The Brighton engines with their unusual colour, curious Stroudley cab, and small domes set well back and crowned by Salter valves, looked very odd when seen for the first time.'

LBSCR turntable problems were evidently solved by the time R. J. Billinton arrived at Brighton for quite soon he introduced a class of 4-4-0 express engines which gave the Brighton line an image more in harmony with that of its northern contemporaries. These were the 'B2' class of 1895, but they were disappointing performers in spite of their looks. There were times throughout the history of the steam locomotive when the magic formula

for matching boiler pressure, heating surface, grate area, cylinder dimensions and wheel diameter seemed to elude even experienced designers.

Lessons learned from the 'B2s' and some later modified engines led to Billinton's much more successful 'B4' express 4-4-0s. Ten engines of this class of 33 were built at Brighton and the rest by Sharp, Stewart & Co. No 70, *Holyrood*, ran from Victoria to Brighton with a test train of three Pullmans and a van in 48min 41sec on 26 July 1903, an average of 63.4mph, with a top speed of 90mph at Horley. This was a response to various schemes for a high-speed electric railway from London to Brighton. The LBSC was already investigating electrification for its suburban services, with long-term thoughts of an electric main line, but it was wisely taking its time. Electric services to Brighton began 30 years later. Since then the best time shown in the public timetables has been 55min. The route provides no opportunity for continuous high speed until after Croydon and faster regular timings would be unrealistic.

In the early years of the Billinton regime Brighton Works were busy with his tank engines, the first of his own design being an 0-4-4. Later he went to six coupled wheels and the trailing bogie was replaced by a radial axle. Billinton designed several series of 0-6-2 radial tanks with wheel diameters of 4ft 6in, 5ft and 5ft 6in, the larger engines being primarily for passenger work, of which there was plenty suited to tank engines on the LBSCR. He also added to the stock of 0-6-0 goods tender engines, but these were built outside at Vulcan Foundry.

If already known as a 'tank engine line' to those who lived in its area, this aspect of the 'Brighton' only became familiar in wider circles when D. Earle Marsh succeeded Billinton in 1905. Marsh's first design, however, was his celebrated Atlantic, described by Dendy Marshall in his official *History of the Southern Railway* as 'a huge 4-4-2 express engine . . . which was a copy of those in use on the Great Northern Railway' (Marsh had been assistant to Ivatt at Doncaster). Five came out in 1905/6, and six more were built in 1911/12, this second batch being superheated. Later generations have associated the Atlantics with the Newhaven boat trains, on which duty they hung on into BR days, losing it only when electric locomotives took it over in 1948. Before the LBSC main line electrifications of the 1930s, however, the Atlantics did excellent work on all the principal passenger services. Innumerable photographs show them on the 'Southern Belle.'

Below: **Billinton's 'B4s' amply made up for the deficiencies of the 'B2s'. No 52, at Brighton in 1899, was named *Siemens* at the time of this picture, but became *Sussex* in 1908.**
Bucknall Collection/IAL

Right: **'B4' No 70, *Holyrood,* is celebrated for a high-speed run to Brighton as a riposte to proposals for new electric railways to Sussex.** LPC/IAL

Below right: **No 54, *Princess Royal,* of Class B4 enters Clapham Junction with the 11.40 Victorial-Brighton about 1908.** *Photograph by the late E. T. Vyse, by courtesy of J. H. Price*

Above left: **Billinton's Class E4 0-6-2T was a development of his 'E3' goods tank built specifically for passenger service. No 561, *Walberton,* came out in 1901.** *IAL*

Left: **An 'E4' with British Rail livery and numbering. No 32508 was originally No 508, *Bognor*.** *M. R. Galley*

Top: **Marsh Class H1 Atlantic No 39 at Brighton in 1920. It was named *La France* in 1913 when the French President made a State Visit to Britain.** *A. B. MacLeod*

Above: **Marsh 'I3' class 4-4-2T No 21 on the 'Southern Belle'. This was the first of a famous class and is seen with its original short smokebox and 'B4' type chimney.** *IAL*

Top: **A 'Terrier' as Works Shunter and 'D' class 0-4-2T No 271 (formerly *Eridge*) outside Brighton mpd.** *Bucknall Collection/IAL*

Above: **In Marsh's day road competition was already making itself felt in rural areas and the company's answer was the rail motor. Two were ordered from Beyer, Peacock in 1905, Nos 1 (illustrated) and 2.** *Madgwick Collection/IAL*

Right: **Rail motor No 1 running trials near Lewes.** *Madgwick Collection/IAL*

Marsh then used the 4-4-2 wheel arrangement in some suburban tank engines, but they were disappointing performers. He had decided, however, on a version for express passenger traffic with 6ft 9in wheels, the first of which appeared as Class I3 in 1907. Subsequent engines of the class had 6ft 7½in dia wheels and a number of them were superheated. The 'I3s' were the first express passenger tank engines in Great Britain and their success in this role was immediate. They also had an impact outside their own territory. When the superheated No 23 began through running between Brighton and Rugby with the 'Sunny South Special' in 1908 the LNWR authorities were much impressed by its economy in fuel and water consumption in comparison with one of George Whale's saturated steam 'Precursor' 4-4-0s. Whale forthwith designed a 4-4-0 with superheater, soon to become famous as the 'George the Fifth' class.

The 'I3s' were smart-looking, but less impressive visually at the head of the 'Southern Belle' than the Atlantics. But probably their records in the statistical and financial returns gave more pleasure to the authorities. Schoolboys in the 1920s who never saw the Brighton line knew the Marsh 4-4-2 tanks from a Bassett-Lowke 'O'-gauge model, which most of them thought represented the 'I3' which had impressed the LNWR. The catalogue blurb implied that this was so without actually saying as much. This illusion was shattered in later years when it was discovered that the No 11 on the side tanks belonged to a relatively undistinguished 'I2'.

Marsh left his mark on the LBSCR in another way by adopting an umber livery in place of Stroudley's yellow. Even the popular newspapers of the day noticed and lamented the change while writers ever since have tried with varying success to explain what this remarkable colour actually looked like. It can, of course, still be seen on the preserved Stroudley engine *Gladstone* in the National Railway Museum at York, and it still gleams on its home ground in the model of the smaller-wheeled 0-4-2 *Como* in the Brighton museum, rescued a few years ago from the archaeology section and placed more appropriately among reminders of Brighton's past as a seaside resort.

It was in Marsh's day, too, that the LBSC management became concerned about unremunerative local services. In the London area electrification was seen as an answer. For other areas Marsh adopted the push-pull rail motor as a unit that would be economical to run and thus able to provide more frequent services, which it was hoped would attract more traffic. Marsh ordered two steam and two petrol railcars in 1905. The steam cars went into trial service between Brighton and Worthing, then between Brighton and Eastbourne, before being shedded at St Leonards for the Eastbourne-St Leonards service. Here they were joined by the petrol cars, which had been given a spell of working on the Kemp Town branch . The petrol cars were not popular with the public but there seemed to be a future for steam push-pulls, although the original cars were under-powered. Marsh converted

Top: **Marsh's first 4-6-2T, No 325, *Abergavenny.*** In Southern livery, as seen here, the name has been removed. *P. Ransome-Wallis*

Above: No 3, one of two petrol-driven railcars acquired by the LBSC from Dick, Kerr in 1905. *Bucknall Collection/IAL*

Above right: No 326, *Bessborough,* was turned out after Marsh had retired. With No 325 it formed the LBSC's Class J, but differed from its sister engine in having Walschaerts valve gear. *IAL*

Right: Conductor rails for electric traction have already been laid at Brighton as 'J' class 4-6-2T leaves with a fast train to London Bridge. *P. Ransome-Wallis*

Above left: **The Brighton line's last locomotive engineer, L. B. Billinton, introduced the Baltic type for the principal trains. His Class L 4-6-4T No 327 *Charles C. Macrae,* is at Brighton in 1920.** *A. B. MacLeod*

Left: **Cross-country turns provided work for the handsome 'J' class tanks for some years after electrification between London and the Sussex Coast. No 2326 heads the 'Sunny South Special' near Falmer in 1936.** *C. C. B. Herbert*

Above: **Towards the end of the 'big tank' era on the Brighton line, the principal duties were shared with a batch of Southern Railway 'King Arthur' 4-6-0s specially built with six-wheel tenders for the Central Section. No 797, *Sir Blamor de Ganis,* passes Patcham with the down 'Southern Belle'.** *IAL*

some 'Terriers' to form what the LBSC called 'motors' in conjunction with coaches of the type popularly called 'Balloons' but modified internally and equipped with driving compartments from which the locomotive was controlled in one direction of running by an electro-pneumatic system. A Brighton-Worthing motor service with this equipment was begun in 1905. Four 2-car motors were built for the same service in 1911 and in due course this type of train was to be seen all over the system. Other motor services operated from Brighton were to East Grinstead and on the Dyke branch. Some 'D' class tanks were modified for these duties as well as 'Terriers'.

Towards the close of Marsh's period in office, Brighton Works turned out the first of a new express passenger tank engine class, this time a 4-6-2 with outside cylinders. Wheel diameter was 6ft 7½in as in the 'I3s' but the wheel arrangement allowed a considerably larger boiler. The

first engine, No 325, *Abergavenny,* had Stephenson's link motion inside valve gear but the second, No 326, *Bessborough,* was equipped with Walschaerts outside valve gear. These two engines appeared in 1910 and 1912 respectively, *Bessborough* not being completed until after Marsh had retired.

In the last independent years of the LBSCR a Billinton was in charge again at Brighton Works, this time L. B. Billinton, son of R. J. The line was now commanding respect as the home of 'big tank' engines (to some the I3s had looked like terriers among greyhounds when compared with main line motive power on other lines). L. B. Billinton rounded things off with his massive 4-6-4 express passenger tank engines of Class L. The first two were turned out in April 1914. Then came a gap during the war years until production of the other five engines in the class was resumed in 1921/22. They performed on the crack trains to Brighton, Eastbourne and Hastings until these services were electrified, although from 1926 they worked alongside a batch of Southern Railway 4-6-0s of the 'King Arthur' class which were built with 6-wheel tenders for operation on the former LBSC main lines. It was a pleasant gesture to entrust the last steam train to Brighton and the last steam 'Southern Belle' to Billinton Baltics. After electrification little work remained for such powerful machines and in 1934 it was decided to convert them into tender engines for service on the longer Southern Railway main lines.

L. B. Billinton also gave the Brighton line its first Moguls for freight traffic, departing from the inside-cylinder 0-6-0 formula which all the other CMEs had followed for the heavier goods duties. Seventeen were built between 1913 and 1921. Freight remained steam-hauled on the Southern's electrified lines until diesels took over in BR days and so the 'K' class Moguls had a long innings, upholding the traditions of Brighton Works to the end.

Top: When 'King Arthur' No 800, *Sir Meleaus de Lile,* was caught near Earlswood in 1929, there were still American-style clerestory-roofed Pullmans in the 'Belle's' formation. *IAL*

Above: A line-up of large tanks at the north end of the 'New Shed' at Brighton mpd. This was a familiar sight in steam days as engines waited to back into the station to take their trains. Class L No 328 heads the parade, with Class J No 325 next to it and another Class L at the rear. *A. B. MacLeod*

Left: With only three electric locomotives on the Central Section of the Southern Railway, freight long remained steam-hauled. L. B. Billinton's 'K' class 2-6-0s appeared on the eve of World War 1. When No 2343 was photographed at Brighton the Southern Railway was on the threshold of nationalisation, with World War 2 behind it. *Author*

5. Electrification

Electrification on the LBSCR began with the South London line from London Bridge to Victoria in 1909. The 15kV single-phase ac system with overhead contact wire that was chosen was already being used on main lines on the Continent, and eventual electrification to Brighton was in prospect from the early days. But the LBSC Board wisely did not take the plunge at once, and did not feel itself seriously threatened by the promoters of a scheme to build an entirely new railway from London to Brighton on which high-speed electric trains would make the journey in half an hour, with one stop en route.

The proposals for a London & Brighton Electric Railway were outlined in a booklet published in 1902, which announced that powers to construct the line were to be applied for in the next session of Parliament. Much of its content was an attack on the supposed lethargy of the London, Brighton & South Coast, and it was claimed that there was no town of the size and importance of Brighton in the United Kingdom that had to depend on the 'vagaries of one railway to connect it with the outer world.' The proposed line was to run in an almost straight course from a London terminus in Lupus Street, Westminster, to a Brighton terminal in Queen's Square, at the opposite end of Queen's Road to the LBSC station and closer to the sea. There would be stations at Beddington, Redhill, and Haywards Heath, and the plans included an electric tramway connecting Redhill with Reigate. Rather more than 19 miles of the route would be in tunnel. Gradients would be 'such that the highest speeds can be obtained at the minimum cost of energy', and the energy was to come from a generating station at Three Bridges of '10,000 horsepower capacity.' Power was to be fed to the trains from a 'ribbon' between the rails.

The imagination of the artist who illustrated the booklet soared high. Lupus Street station was shown as an enlarged Charing Cross with a splendid crop of turrets and pinnacles. The Brighton terminus looked like one of the palatial hotels one sometimes sees on Continental luggage labels, with balustraded terraces and a fountain in the forecourt. The trains which would 'enable the community at large to get at one of the most healthy, fashionable and prosperous resorts in the kingdom, in the quickest possible time' were 5-car sets with a streamlined nose reminiscent of the *coupe-vent* smokebox of the early PLM. This accoutrement was described in the text as a 'windscreen.' An illustration showed one of the trains speeding past an admiring group including one gentleman in a top hat and another in sporting tweeds,

propping himself on a shooting stick. An unflattering representation of a London to Brighton steam train on another page depicted four coaches headed by an outside-cylinder 4-4-0 with a large headlamp, looking as if it had been acquired cheaply from some Outpost of Empire and clearly incapable of accomplishing the journey in 30 minutes.

There was to be a regular-interval timetable with trains leaving each terminus every 20 minutes and calling in rotation at one of the intermediate stations which would thus be given an hourly service. Return fares from London or Brighton were to be five shillings (25p) first class and three shillings (15p) third class, with return halves valid for a year. The economies may have been debatable and the faith in the electric traction equipment of the day unduly high, but the scheme foreshadowed ideas that are now familiar, such as the purpose-built high-speed line, and gradients planned to maximise the use of kinetic energy.

There was no rush to invest in the London & Brighton Electric Railway and its Bill was rejected. The promoters' proposals did, however, prod R. J. Billinton into demonstrating what steam could do by the test run of *Holyrood* on 26 July 1903 which has been mentioned in Chapter 4. Like the exploit of *Mallard* on the LNER 35 years later the event was an addition to railway lore but of little significance to the travelling public. The complicated geography of the main line to Brighton for much of its course out of London limits what either steam or electricity has been able to do in reducing the journey time below the hour.

Another abortive scheme was for an underground railway to improve communications between Brighton station and the front. Two routes were proposed; one was from Brighton LBSC to an underground terminus on the front at the end of Russell Street; the other and shorter one was from the southern end of Queens Road to the front at Middle Street. Both these terminal sites were roughly half way between the piers. It may be wondered whether the promoters based their second route on the prospect of the London & Brighton Electric Railway being built to its proposed terminus in Queen's Square. Powers to build the underground line were applied for in 1898 but the Bill soon foundered. It is said to have been carelessly drawn up, with mistakes in local geography and street names that in themselves harmed its credibility.

The LBSC pushed on with suburban electrification, continuing with its plans after the Grouping of 1923, so

Top: An electric 'Brighton fast' formed of 6PUL units speeds past Star Lane on the Quarry Line.   *R. C. Riley*

Above: A Brighton line semi-fast service passes the old Gatwick Airport station, connected by subway with the original 'beehive' airport passenger building.   *R. C. Riley*

Above right: The PUL/PAN combination common to Brighton, Eastbourne and Hastings express services is seen in this view of a Victoria-Brighton non-stop.   *P. J. Sharpe*

Right: Two 4LAV units form a semi-fast leaving Brighton for London.   *IAL*

that by 1929 the overhead wires had reached as far south on the main line as Coulsdon. But for uniformity with the South Western and South Eastern sections of the Southern Railway it had already been decided that the 'Brighton' must change to direct current with third-rail supply. This system, hitherto confined to suburban lines, was the one with which the main line to Brighton was finally electrified.

The decision to electrify to Brighton was taken by the Southern Railway and announced in 1930; and although the company's publicity hailed it as heralding Britain's first electric main line, at boardroom level the scheme was viewed as extending a suburban electrification. Retaining the third-rail had the advantage that existing suburban electric stock could be brought into use for excursion and weekend traffic, with a big saving in the expenditure required for new vehicles.

The lines electrified were from Coulsdon to Brighton (36 miles), along the coast from Brighton to West Worthing (11½ miles), and the Cliftonville curve from Preston Park to Hove. While the work was in progress, colour-light signalling was being extended from Coulsdon to Brighton, forming the longest continuous colour-light section in the country at the time. The resignalling was completed first and brought into use on 16 October 1932. At Brighton a new power box with 225 levers replaced the six mechanical boxes which had controlled the area previously. They had 582 levers between them, the largest being the South box with 240 levers and the West box with 120. Also in the station area was Montpelier Junction box controlling the junction with the east coast line. For many years the junction signals were mounted on the box itself as had been early signalling practice, and the arms for the east coast line were set at

an angle for easy sighting when approaching the station from the Falmer direction.

The area controlled by the new box at Brighton extended to within half-a-mile of Preston Park; to Hove east home signals (semaphores), and to London Road station on the east coast line. A new box at Preston Park took over from the previous Preston Park North and Preston Park South. At Brighton the miniature levers in the frame were electrically interlocked. Elsewhere in the resignalling mechanical interlocking was retained but the levers were fitted with circuit-controllers which acted as switches for operating the colour-light signals and power-operated points too far from the boxes for manual operation. For the most part, however, points continued to be operated through rodding.

Power for electric traction was taken from the Grid and converted to 660V direct current in rectifier substations. The mercury-arc rectifier was just becoming established. Those in the Brighton scheme were rated at 2,500kW but could handle 4,000kW for 5min. All substations were remotely controlled and monitored from the control room at Three Bridges. In the Brighton area they were situated outside the station; at Preston Park and Pangdean on the main line; and at Portslade on the west coast line.

In readiness for electrification the old paint shop of Brighton Works, on the west side of the main line, was converted into a carriage repair and cleaning shed with 12 tracks, seven of them with inspection pits. Certain platforms in Brighton station were lengthened to take 12-car trains and the old bay road, once Platform 4, was abolished, providing extra platform width. The island platform at Hove was lengthened by 17ft to 800ft, and the down platform by 139ft to 787ft (Fig 7).

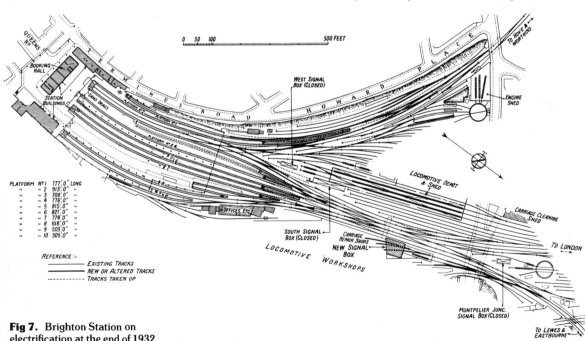

PLATFORM Nº 1 777'.0" LONG
"   "   2 913'.0" "
"   "   3 708'.0" "
"   "   4 716'.0" "
"   "   5 815'.0" "
"   "   6 821'.0" "
"   "   7 774'.0" "
"   "   8 618'.0" "
"   "   9 503'.0" "
"   " 10 305'.0" "

REFERENCE :-
—————— EXISTING TRACKS
—————— NEW or ALTERED TRACKS
- - - - - - - TRACKS TAKEN UP

Fig 7. Brighton Station on electrification at the end of 1932.

Above: **Colour-lights controlled from a modified mechanical signalbox at Hassocks.** *John Scrace*

Below: **Hove 'A' signalbox, at the east end of the station. The colour-light signalling installed at the time of electrification extended to Hove east home signals.** *John Scrace*

New stock was built for express, semi-fast, and all-Pullman services. The 20 6-car units for express traffic comprised two open third motor coaches, each with four 225hp traction motors; three side-corridor coaches; and a Pullman car. There was no corridor connection between units, but since there was a Pullman in each all passengers had access to refreshments. Three 'City Limited' units were similar except for a higher proportion of first class seating.

Semi-fast services were worked by 4-car units of compartment stock. The motorcoaches were powered by two motors of 275hp. One composite vehicle per unit had a side corridor. This was meagre provision for a service which inevitably carried many families with small children, often hot and fractious after a day at the seaside, and competition for the limited space was keen. Success went to those who studied train formations. For the rest — the 'come on George, get in here!' school — it was a disagreeable experience to find themselves trapped once the train was moving, and obliged to spend much of the journey smiling apologetically at fellow passengers suffering harassment from their disgruntled offspring. But this was all in the Brighton line tradition. At least, in the

Below left: **No 2939, one of the last 4LAV survivors, stands beyond a platform barrier in Brighton station on 28 October 1968, over 30 years after its first appearance there.** *John A. M. Vaughan*

Right: **Generations of Brighton electric stock meet in the Brighton platforms on 27 July 1965. A 6PUL unit stands on the left, a 4LAV in the centre, and a train of the 'Brighton Replacement' stock of 1964 (Classes 420/421, originally 4BIG 4CIG) on the right.** *J. A. V. Woods*

Below: **A 4HAL from the west coast line in Brighton's Platform 2 has an unexpected neighbour in Platform 3 in the shape of No 4472, *Flying Scotsman*, on a preservation society special on 17 September 1966.** *John H. Bird*

Above: **A train from the east coast line formed of a 2HAL and a 2BIL passes the power signalbox perched on what remains of the works buildings as it enters Brighton.** *P. J. Sharpe*

Right: **The 'Brighton Belle' in the umber and cream Pullman livery it carried from 1933 until 1969.** *British Rail*

new electric trains, the children could amuse themselves and distract their neighbours by playing with the folding arm-rests with which the non-corridor third class compartments were fitted. These could be used to split the five-a-side seats into modules of two, one, and two, providing interesting opportunities for individuals and groups to signal clearly that they neither had nor desired any connection with the parties next to them. Arm-rests in those days were considered the height of chic, on a par with the tasselled hand-grips in the rear seats of cars which could be gripped to avoid undignified loss of balance when cornering.

The 'Southern Belle' also had to be electrified. The three 5-car sets built for this service were the first electric multiple-unit Pullman trains in the world. As in the express sets, the motorcoaches had four 225hp motors. These vehicles were third class cars; the other three in the unit were two first class and another third. Apart from wartime withdrawal, the five 'Belle' sets were in service until they made their last journeys on 30 April 1972. Throughout their life they retained their original traction motors, which were rewound but not otherwise changed. With eight motors in a 5-car unit, the 'Belle' sets could match the performance of the new express stock for the Brighton line introduced in 1964 with four 250hp motors in a 4-car formation (Classes 420 and 421).

Stopping services on the west coast line between Brighton and West Worthing were worked at first by 3-car suburban sets transferred from the South Western section.

The electrification was inaugurated formally on 30 December 1932. It was an occasion of some civic dignity, with the Lord Mayor of London arriving at Victoria with liveried coachmen and footmen to join the special train and attended by his sword-bearer. The special was formed of a '6-City' unit (ie one of the 6-car sets with Pullman for the 'City Limited'), and it ran non-stop to Worthing via the Cliftonville curve. It then travelled back along the coast to Brighton, where the guests lunched at the Royal Pavilion. Here the Lord Mayor proposed the toast of 'The electrification of the Southern Railway to Brighton', and reflected on the advance of science. In prophetic vein, he forecast that since science knew no last word (of which he quoted the motorcar, the aeroplane, and the wireless as evidence), the steam train might be a museum piece in a few years' time.

Steam took a beating from the correspondent of the *Brighton Herald* in his report of the proceedings. He rejoiced that the electric train had 'got rid of the heavy appearance of the steam train as it has got rid of the smoke and the fire and the loud puffing.' In the electrics

'the oscillation was gentler, more even.' The noise was similarly softened, being 'more akin to the rushing of the wind than to the old "bump and clank".' In later years the 'rushing wind' swelled in volume and set up a doleful moaning sound. The phenomenon was called 'roaring rails' and said to be caused by corrugation of their surface by the repeated passage of motor bogies. Some regular travellers on the Brighton line seemed to develop frequency-selective hearing and could ignore the sound, but it was very noticeable to visitors from north of the Thames familiar only with 'the old bump and clank.'

On 31 December 1932 the last steam-hauled 'Southern Belle' arrived behind 4-6-4T No 333, *Remembrance*. The last steam-hauled main line train slipped into the terminus in the small hours of New Year's Day, 1933, with No 329, *Stephenson*, of the same class at the head. Later in the morning enthusiastic crowds welcomed the arrival of the first electric 'Southern Belle'. Southern Railway top brass emerged from the Pullmans,

and with them were members of the London Madrigal Group who had given a recital en route to demonstrate that the exceptionally quiet running of the stock made it possible to have such a concert on a railway train for the first time.

The Southern must have felt it had scored a public relations triumph when a few days later the proceedings at the Court of Quarter Sessions in Brighton were halted while the Chairman, 'amid all the solemnities of wig and gown', sought leave to congratulate 'this ever-advancing borough upon the introduction of a service of electric trains between the greatest metropolis in the world and the best British coastal town.' At Shoreham the event was commemorated by the striking of a medal depicting an electric train on one side and the town's ancient church on the other.

The new electric train service was fast and frequent. Standardised departure times for the principal London-Brighton train services had been introduced as early as 1865 but now the practice was extended to all trains outside the rush hours. Non-stops making the journey in 60min left Brighton for Victoria from 9am to 4pm and 6pm to midnight. There were two semi-fasts an hour, one to Victoria and one to London Bridge. The Victoria trains called at Preston Park, Haywards Heath, Redhill, East Croydon, and Clapham Junction. Those to London Bridge called additionally at Three Bridges and Horley, with a stop at New Cross Gate instead of Clapham Junction. Two stopping trains an hour ran alternately to Victoria and London Bridge, and there was a stopping train every 15min along the coast line to West Worthing. Hove now had an hourly fast train to London

Top: **A London-bound 'Belle' approaches Burgess Hill on 28 April 1972, with the ridge of the South Downs visible in the background.** *John Scrace*

Above: **A 5BEL off its track. Unit No 3053 crosses the London Road Viaduct, Brighton, after a sally on to the east coast line with a Railway Correspondence & Travel Society excursion on 4 April 1972.** *John Scrace*

Above right: **A Portsmouth Harbour-Brighton train passes Hove 'B' box, now removed, at the west end of the station.** *John Scrace*

Right: **Semaphores still rule at Shoreham-by-Sea.** *John Scrace*

provided by the Worthing-Victoria service via the Cliftonville curve.

After the euphoria came the grumbles. Way back in 1894 John Pendleton had written in *Our Railways* of the imperious habits of the Brighton first class passenger, who when displeased was prone to call the guard or, in extreme cases, to demand the head of the stationmaster on a charger. Forty years later this formidable personage's descendants were content to write to the local press with their complaints. It was claimed that the first class carriages were constructed so that it was impossible to avoid a draught; that passengers, having no means of regulating the heating system, were either roasted or frozen at the whim of railway officials; and that if refuge was sought in the third class, where the

compartments were considered less draughty, there were other discomforts because the seats were 'unsuitably dimensioned for persons of average size' while the jolting of the coach made reading difficult. Residents of Preston Park complained that the fast trains flashed through their station, obliging them to take the semi-fasts unless they journeyed into central Brighton.

The electrics found an unexpected champion in the Manager of the Lido cinema at Hove. Whispers were now circulating that the new trains interfered with the 'talkies'. He hastened to squash the rumour in an interview with the press. 'We welcome the electrification of the line' he said, 'for not only will it bring more and more people to Hove but it will remove the nuisance of the "Puffing Billy". The one thing we have suffered from is the letting off of steam by engines standing in the siding just outside the cinema.'

After an unlucky start in which severe weather demonstrated the vulnerability of the third-rail to ice and snow the service settled down and electric trains became as much a part of the Brighton scene as the Palace Pier, with steam trains by the main line to London no more than an heroic theme for the tellers of tales. But it took some time to get used to an electric 'Southern Belle'. For those who enjoyed looking at trains as well as riding in them, locomotive and Pullman Cars were inseparable in the image evoked by the name. The new train had no visible means of propulsion. In the flow of reminiscence that accompanied the withdrawal of the 'Belle' in 1972, staff at Brighton recalled that visitors from the Continent were often puzzled by an electric train with no overhead wires, and on occasions were nearly left behind because they lingered over their farewells on the platform under the impression that 'the engine hasn't come on yet.' A further blow was the change of name to 'Brighton Belle' in 1934. It was sensible now that there was a

'Bournemouth Belle' as well and others to come, but it seemed to link the train with popular Brighton between the piers rather than with the exclusive Brighton of Royal Crescent and Sussex Square. It took some years for the name to acquire a bouquet; by the time the end came nearly 40 years later it was spoken with the reverence accorded to a rare vintage wine.

When the lines from Keymer junction to Lewes, Seaford, Eastbourne, Hastings and Ore were electrified in 1935, the section from Brighton to Lewes was included and so from 7 July in that year the east coast line services from Brighton were worked by electric multiple-units. Steam passenger workings between Brighton and Lewes were then confined to trains serving the East Grinstead and Tunbridge Wells groups of lines. Stopping trains from Brighton ran alternatively to Seaford, and to Eastbourne and Hastings. Passengers from Brighton to

Below: **Below the grassy slopes from which the people of Brighton welcomed their first London trains in 1841, a 4LAV hums towards the coast at Patcham on 26 April 1968.** *John Scrace*

Right: **This picture of a 5BEL unit at Brighton recalls that these Pullman sets carried the same of the train on their 'bows', reinforcing the associations with pleasure steamers which 'Brighton Belle' evoked in many minds.** *John Scrace*

Below right: **In their last years 4COR sets from the LSWR 'direct Portsmouth' route worked in the Brighton area. Unit No 3132 is at Portslade on a West Worthing-Brighton service.** *John Scrace*

Eastbourne and Hastings could also change at Lewes into one of the fast trains from London with a wait of only five minutes on Lewes station.

Although the new electrification affected primarily the London-Eastbourne-Hastings service, it had its effect on the London-Brighton trains. The new express stock comprised 6-car sets in which one car had a pantry compartment from which light refreshments could be served. These were the '6PAN' units, and they ran coupled to the earlier 6-car sets with Pullman ('6PUL') built for the Brighton electrification. From that time onwards 6PUL/6PAN formations were seen both on London-Eastbourne-Hastings and London-Brighton fast services.

Hove gained an extra morning business service to London. The 7.22am ex-Worthing called there en route to Brighton, where it reversed and continued on the main line to Haywards Heath, to be attached there to an up Eastbourne train. There was a similar return working to Hove and Worthing via Brighton in the evening.

Continuing with its electrification programme, the Southern Railway converted the Waterloo-Portsmouth service in July 1937 and a year later did the same for the ex-LBSC Portsmouth route via Horsham. This reached the coast at Ford, and so the work included extending electrification along the west coast line from West Worthing to Ford and over the Littlehampton branch. When the scheme was inaugurated in July 1938 the hourly fast trains from London to Worthing via the Cliftonville curve and Hove were extended to Littlehampton. West coast line electric services from Brighton now comprised two all-stations trains an hour to West Worthing, one continuing to Littlehampton and Bognor; an hourly semi-fast to Portsmouth Harbour serving Hove, Shoreham, Worthing Central and slow thence to Portsmouth, and an hourly fast Portsmouth calling only at Hove, Shoreham, Worthing Central,

Barnham, Chichester, Fratton, Portsmouth Town and Portsmouth Harbour.

In the postwar years the first new trains built specifically for the Brighton line were the 4-car units of Classes 420 and 421. When introduced in 1964 these inaugurated a new practice for Southern electric stock in that instead of there being a motorcoach at each end of the formation the unit composition was driving trailer, motorcoach (with four traction motors), trailer, and second driving trailer. In Class 420 the trailer was a buffet car. By this time the Pullman Car Company had been absorbed by British Rail and the practice of running Pullmans as catering vehicles in trains of ordinary stock was dropped. If the fare was less varied and enticing than in the Pullmans, it was an improvement on the tea and biscuits offered in the '6PANs.'

The 'Brighton Belle' Pullman sets were stored during World War 2 but returned to service in 1948/9. BR acquisition of Pullman shares began in 1954, but the 'Belle' sets continued in the traditional umber and cream Pullman livery until they underwent internal renovation in 1968-69. From this they emerged in BR's Pullman livery of blue and grey. By now the end was near for a Brighton tradition of some 60 years. Danger ahead was sensed when it was announced that kippers were to be removed from the Pullman menu. A protest movement was headed by Sir Laurence (now Lord) Olivier and the kippers were reprieved. Hope rose that the train itself might be spared but this was not to be. The Pullman sets made their last runs on 30 April 1972. The final journey from Victoria to Brighton at 23.00 was a 'Champagne Special'. This was very much a show business occasion for the 'Belles' had always been popular with the theatrical profession. The last train down at night sometimes witnessed unusual incidents among its emotional clientele, such as the occasion when a leading lady inverted her plate of mixed grill over the head of a

Left: The 09.14 Brighton-Eastbourne on 27 April 1971 is formed of 4COR unit No 3106, seen entering Falmer. *John Scrace*

Right: A 4CIG unit in its original all-blue livery heads the 15.00 Victoria to Brighton where the line emerges from Braypool Cutting at Patcham on 30 May 1968. *John Scrace*

Below: Rail blue and grey has replaced plain blue on 4CIG No 7308, seen leaving Balcombe tunnel with a Littlehampton-Victoria service on 15 June 1968. *John Scrace*

theatrical agent. 'More like a club than a train' mused conductor John Verral, affectionately recalling the idiosyncracies of some of his customers. A reporter travelling on this last trip collected nostalgic comments from the stars on board, most of whom thought that this was not an occasion to dwell on the occasional rough riding of the ageing Pullmans, but Robert Morley was less reticent. 'It's a particularly jerky train, and always has been' he grumbled, and he shed no tears for an end which he saw as part of the natural order of things.

Thus the 'Belle' passed into history. A proposal to offer special menus in the buffets of ordinary trains running at the same times as the 'Belle' services came to nothing. At Victoria, however, the name lived for on a time in a 'Brighton Belle' buffet that took the place of a former station cafeteria.

There was a now half-forgotten episode in the career of the 'Belle' cars in the 1960s. A company known as Charter Trains Limited hired a 5BEL set for running 'Regency Belle' weekend trips from Victoria to Brighton at an all-in fare of seven guineas covering dinner and dancing at the Royal Albion Hotel and the opportunity for what was described as 'a mild flutter' at the tables. The train left Victoria at 19.15 on Saturdays and

Above: 'Battle of Britain' Pacific No 34088 waits to leave Victoria with the 'Regency Belle' night-life special to Brighton on one of the occasions when five locomotive-hauled Pullmans with a full brake at each end replaced a 5BEL unit.   *G. D. King*

Left: The ubiquitous 4VEPs (Class 423) came to the Brighton area in the 1970s. In this picture unit No 7783 stands in Platform 1 at Brighton on 9 February 1978 awaiting departure to Bognor Regis.   *L. A. Nixon*

Sundays, returning at 02.15 on the Sunday or Monday morning. A 'typical English breakfast' was served on the way home to those who felt able to cope with egg, bacon and sausage between 02.15 and arrival home at 03.30. Regency trappings were much in evidence. Six hostesses in Regency costume attended the travellers, and some of the traditional Pullman decorative features were temporarily disguised with clip-on Regency decor. Modernity returned at Brighton, where a fleet of cars was waiting to take the excursionists to the hotel. Tickets were specially designed and printed in gold and maroon. The train first ran on 28 March 1964 but only lasted for a few weeks. On some occasions locomotive-hauled Pullmans were used with a Bulleid Pacific at the head, as seen in an illustration in this chapter.

After electrification of the London-Brighton services the public timetable schedule of the non-stop trains long remained at 60min although working times were shorter. In 1939 the 5pm from London Bridge was allowed 56min. Introduction of the Class 420/1 sets in 1964 was followed in July 1967 by new timetables which showed a standard 55min for the non-stop services. In 1979, however, the classic Brighton non-stop disappeared. To meet changing patterns of traffic and population all trains called at East Croydon and the public time with this one stop became 58min.

6. Secondary Services and Freight

Although a London to Brighton route crossing the South Downs near Shoreham was rejected in favour of Rennie's 'direct' line, rails were laid through the Shoreham Gap when the branch from Shoreham to Itchingfield Junction was built. From 1 October 1861 this gave access to Horsham and onwards to London via Three Bridges. An alternative route from Horsham to London became available when Horsham was connected with Leatherhead on 1 March 1867. There was now an approximation to the route from London to Brighton which had been proposed by Robert Stephenson (Fig 8). The LBSC used to publish its timetables in the local press, and the trains by this route appeared under the heading 'From Brighton to London by way of Steyning, Henfield, Horsham and Dorking.' In 1869 six up services were shown, two of them first and second class only and not calling at Dorking. The best time was 2hr 42min. The basic service consisted of Brighton-Horsham locals plus freight and livestock in great variety. Extra trains for livestock were run on Steyning market days. Horsebox

traffic at Cowfold in the early 1920s was the heaviest at any LBSC station. All stations on the branch dealt with milk and perishables by passenger train; all except Bramber had yards busy with miscellaneous country traffic. Industry was served as well. The Sussex Brick Works at Southwater despatched 40 wagons of bricks a day, while receiving regular consignments of coal. Beeding Cement Works also sent its output by rail, and some works traffic continued even after the branch was closed to passengers in 1966. The Shoreham-Beeding section, 2½ miles, was kept open and operated as a siding for delivering gypsum to the works, then owned by Blue Circle Industries Limited. The gypsum was usually ordered weekly and supplied from Battle in East Sussex, travelling to Beeding via the yards at Norwood and Brighton. This traffic continued until 21 April 1980 when a consignment of 305 tonnes which had been despatched from Battle on 18 April was delivered at the works. From that date the gypsum was sent by road, although the connection at Shoreham with the line to

Fig 8. Main and secondary routes to Brighton, with dates of opening.

Brighton-Shoreham	1840
London-Brighton	1841
Brighton-Lewes	1846
Wivelsfield-Lewes	1847
Three Bridges-Horsham	1848
Three Bridges-East Grinstead	1855
Lewes-Uckfield	1858
Shoreham-Itchingfield Junction	1861
East Grinstead-Tunbridge Wells	1866
Groombridge-Uckfield	1868
Lewes-East Grinstead	1882
Horsted Keynes-Haywards Heath	1883
Ashurst Spur (Ashurst Junction to Groombridge-Uckfield line)	1914

Above: **Partridge Green station buildings in 1967, a year after closure of the Shoreham-Itchingfield Junction line. Partridge Green was the terminus from July to October 1861.** *John A. M. Vaughan*

Left: **Steyning signalbox. From 1964 to closure of the branch in 1966 this was the only signalbox remaining open on the line.** *Madgwick Collection/IAL*

Above right: **BR Standard Class 4 2-6-4T No 80085 arrives at Brighton with a train from Horsham on 8 April 1964.** *Bryan H. Jackson*

Beeding was maintained. Before 1980 varying amounts of gypsum had been received by rail from British Gypsum Limited at Burton on Trent.

With the coast so near, excursions were a feature from the earliest years of the line. A fortnight after it was opened as far as Partridge Green on 1 July 1861 the people of Henfield celebrated the advent of the railway with an excursion to Portsmouth and the Isle of Wight. A month later many local children probably made their first trip by train when the annual school treat was an outing to Brighton and visit to the Chain Pier. After World War 1 and the Grouping the route via Horsham and Shoreham began to come into its own as an alternative to the main line to Brighton for excursions from the London area, from Reading via the Guildford-Horsham branch, and from further afield. These operations brought more main line locomotives to the Shoreham-Horsham line, although local services in the 1920s often produced 'Gladstones'. Otherwise motive power was drawn from a variety of small LBSC tank classes and 0-6-0 goods engines. An interesting source of variety was provided by running-in turns from Brighton Works to Steyning. One of the few through workings from Victoria to Brighton by this route was the 16.05 down, which on one occasion in 1915 was seen at Steyning headed by Baltic tank No 327, *Charles C. Macrae*. On the eve of World War 2 four trains from Brighton actually worked through to London,

but two of them made such long stops at Horsham that they could hardly be regarded as through trains. The other two stopped at Horsham for 14min and 16min respectively, reaching Victoria in 2hr 49min and 3hr 5min. There were five through down trains, but again only two made relatively short stops at Horsham; one of them was still the 16.05 from Victoria.

Electrification from Shoreham to Horsham was included in the Southern's electrification plans after World War 2 but was overshadowed by larger projects and never carried out. It would have provided an all-electric alternative to the London-Brighton main line between Three Bridges and Brighton, much less circuitous than the present one via the Mid-Sussex line and Ford. On the other hand, when diversions from the main line south of Three Bridges are necessary today, the Mid-Sussex route enables diverted Brighton trains to provide Worthing and Littlehampton with through London services.

On the secondary route to London east of the main line, via Lewes, East Grinstead and Oxted, there were five through trains each way daily towards the end of the 19th century. Journey times were about three hours and the trains called at nearly all stations south of Croydon. By 1910 through coaches were being run between Brighton and London via Lewes, Uckfield and Groombridge. In the up direction the coaches left

Above: **Ex-LBSC Class E4 0-6-2T No 32469 (formerly**
Beachy Head) **calls at Shoreham-by-Sea with a Brighton to**
Horsham local in April 1960. *John C. Baker*

Right: **BR 2-6-2T No 41301 leaves Brighton for Horsham in**
March 1961. *Brian Haresnape*

Brighton at 08.03 on a Tunbridge Wells train, from which
they were detached at Groombridge. Here they were
attached, together with others that had come from
Eastbourne, to a Tunbridge Wells-Victoria train and
arrived in London at 10.38. The down service consisted
of coaches for Brighton attached to the 15.45 from
Victoria to Tunbridge Wells, again in company with
Eastbourne coaches. The train ran non-stop to
Groombridge and the Brighton coaches completed their
journey on the 16.43 from Tunbridge Wells, reaching
Brighton at 18.11.

In July 1914 the Ashurst spur, avoiding Groombridge,
was opened and by 1915 two trains each way between
Brighton and London by the Uckfield route made use of
it. In the service curtailments later in the war the Brighton
and Eastbourne trains by this route were again combined
but they now joined and separated at Eridge. After the
war train services were progressively increased and
improved, including those on the secondary routes, and
in the first year of Grouping there were six through trains
each way between Brighton and London via Lewes and
East Grinstead. There was also a London service running
between Brighton and East Grinstead via Haywards

Fig 9. Brighton junctions and signalboxes.

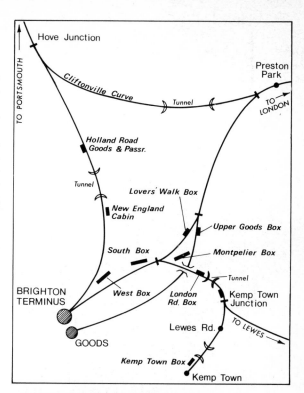

Heath and Horsted Keynes, consisting of three up and five down trains. Two through trains each way travelled via Uckfield and the Ashurst spur.

By the 1860s Brighton was large enough to have a branch within its own boundaries. Thomas Read Kemp, one of the Lords of the Manor of Brighton, had developed an estate of large houses in the later 1820s on land he owned on the East Cliff. Building was spread over some 20 years, and was accompanied by the spread eastwards of more modest dwellings and shops on the landward side of the imposing residences. The whole of this area came to be known as Kemp Town, although originally the name was given only to the estate itself. In 1864 the LBSC obtained powers to build a branch to serve this part of Brighton and the line was opened on 2 August 1869. Leaving the east coast line at Kemp Town junction, 76ch from Brighton station (Fig 9), the branch was only 1 mile 32ch long but in that short distance traversed a viaduct of 28 arches and passed through a tunnel 1,024yd long at the approach to Kemp Town station. This terminus was off the Eastern Road, a thoroughfare parallel with Marine Parade but just under a quarter of a mile inland. The station was little more than half a mile east of the Old Steine and the Pavilion, but the

Left: The Shoreham-Horsham line connected with the Horsham-Guildford branch and provided a route to Brighton for excursions from the Western Region via Reading. 'Q1' class No 33022 pilots a Kidderminster to Brighton excursion on to the Horsham line at Peasmarsh Junction, near Guildford. *A. A. Livesey*

Centre left: Falmer station was the first out of Brighton on the east coast line until the opening of London Road (Brighton) in 1877. *Lens of Sutton*

Bottom left: The signalbox on Falmer station platform in 1971. *John Scrace*

Right: Brighton mpd in 1960. Brighton signalbox is on the right, and in the middle distance the east coast line curves away on the London Road viaduct. *John Scrace*

Below: Class 4 2-6-0 No 76057 crosses the London Road viaduct with the 11.55 Brighton to Tonbridge on 25 January 1958. *G. Daniels*

distance by rail from Brighton station was no less than 2 miles 28ch, the route being almost a semicircle. None the less, the line was welcomed locally and the *Brighton Gazette* observed in its issue of 5 August 1869: 'The Kemp Town branch of the Brighton Railway was opened on Monday and trains now run at intervals every day. The station is in close proximity to Brighton College, and the line will be found a great convenience to residents and visitors at the east end of the town.' The initial service was nine trains each way with a journey time of 10 minutes.

The viaduct, with a maximum height above ground of 52ft, crossed the Lewes Road, and a station with this name was opened on the Brighton side of the viaduct on 1 September 1873. To this point the branch was double-track, the station having an island platform and a platform on the up side with the station buildings. There was also a goods yard with six sidings and a further short siding serving a coal merchant's yard. Beyond these installations the line became single-track for the rest of the distance over the viaduct and into the terminus. On emerging from the tunnel into the station the cutting

widened to accommodate a yard of some 17 sidings and a number of sheds. The station had a single platform with a bay, and a run-round loop.

From 1 October 1877 the LBSC provided another facility for eastern Brighton with the opening of London Road station on the east coast line, between Brighton station and Kemp Town junction. In its early days London Road was serviced principally by the Kemp Town trains but all east coast line trains call there today. There were no freight facilities, the station being only 60ch from the Brighton terminus and its goods station. Architecturally the station building was in a similar style to Kemp Town and West Worthing but since the station is above road level it is graced additionally with a wide flight of steps leading to the entrance.

The Kemp Town branch acquired a short-lived halt at Hartington Road on 1 January 1906. Access was by a cinder path from the road or from Upper Wellington Road, a cul de sac bounded at its eastern end by the railway. The halt closed in April 1911.

Beginning with nine trains each way, the service built up to an average of 17 by 1880. Until the introduction of

Below left: A Class 33 diesel waits in Platform 9 at Brighton on an Oxted line train alongside a 2BIL unit with a Seaford service on Platform 8. This view shows the shorter span of the station roof next to the two main spans over the west coast and main line platforms. *John A. M. Vaughan*

Right: The Kemp Town 'motor' formed of 'Terrier' No 647 and a 'balloon' coach enters Brighton about 1922. *Madgwick Collection/IAL*

Centre right: Kemp Town station with a 'D' tank on a train of four-wheelers. *LPC/IAL*

Bottom right: Kemp Town tunnel and signalbox. *IAL*

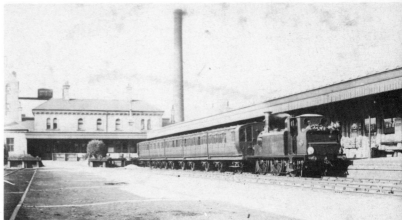

Left: Interior of a 'balloon' coach converted for use in push-pull 'motor' trains. *Madgwick Collection/IAL*

Below: 'Terrier' No 64 (later 664) commemorates the early town planning venture of Thomas Read Kemp on Brighton's East Cliff. *IAL*

Right: By the late 1960s Kemp Town's train service consisted of one daily goods, consisting here of a solitary coal wagon. Diesel-electric shunter No D3220 is in charge of the convoy on 10 July 1969. *John A. M. Vaughan*

Below right: Kemp Town yard is shunted by No D3669 on 3 April 1969. *J. M. Tolson*

Left: **The Kemp Town branch attracted various excursions in the 1950s and 1960s. On the left of this picture 'Terrier' No 32636 (***Fenchurch,*** now preserved on the Bluebell Railway) has left the old Kemp Town platform at Brighton with LBSC push-pull set No 727 for a trip down the branch on 5 October 1952 in connection with the Brighton Works centenary celebrations. A Railway Correspondence & Travel Society special Pullman train at the main line platform is headed by LBSC Atlantic No 32424,** *Beachy Head.* *IAL*

Below left: **Final closure of the Kemp Town branch came with the end of freight traffic. On 26 June 1971 enthusiasts had a last opportunity to travel over the line on farewell journeys operated by Class 206 demu No 1205.** *C. S. Heaps*

Above: **Kemp Town Station exterior in 1969.** *J. M. Tolson*

Centre right: **Similar in style to other local LBSC stations, London Road is distinguished by its flight of steps leading from the pavement to the booking hall.** *Lens of Sutton*

Right: **London Road platforms, looking east towards the tunnel under the high ground on which the Ditchling Road crosses the line.** *Lens of Sutton*

Marsh's 'motors' the trains were usually 5-coach close-coupled sets worked by 'Terrier' tanks although the 'D1' 0-4-2s appeared occasionally. At the busiest periods the branch was worked by two engines in steam, and there were actually 18 trains each way on the branch in 1932, its last year of passenger service. Lewes Road and Kemp Town stations were closed to passenger traffic on 31 December in that year. Goods traffic continued, but from 29 July 1933 the branch ceased to be worked as a section and became a siding with one engine in steam. Coal traffic to the yards at Lewes Road and Kemp Town continued until 1971 but on 26 June in that year this traffic was transferred to Hove. Various enthusiasts' passenger specials had worked over the branch since World War 2, and on the last day BR provided a final opportunity to travel over it by running a service of hourly trips by 'Tadpole' demu No 1205.

High in the Downs to the west of Brighton there is a long, deep hollow called the Dyke. Legend claims that it was excavated by the Devil with the intention of letting the sea through the rampart of hills to flood the Weald beyond. Luckily he was seen at work by an old woman, who had the presence of mind to put a lighted lantern in her cottage window. The Devil thought it was the first glow of the rising sun, and as the dawn is hostile to the Powers of Darkness he abandoned his task in haste and dudgeon. For many years the high ground he was obliged to leave untouched has been a popular place of excursion for visitors to Brighton, commanding fine views over the Weald, the Downs and the sea.

The horse-drawn vehicles that took early excursionists to the Dyke were slow and often expensive. A round trip from Brighton by waggonette took three hours – an hour each way on the journey and an hour at the Dyke. There seemed to be an opening for a railway, not only for the excursion traffic but for possible housing development at the summit. The Brighton & Dyke Railway Company was formed, and in its prospectus spoke of an estimated annual traffic of at least 273,000 persons, with 10,000 visitors on Bank Holidays. 'I apprehend that when the line is opened a considered number of residences will be erected round the terminus', wrote the company's engineer in his contribution to this document. The Act of incorporation was granted on 2 August 1877, and on 1 September 1887 the line was opened from a junction with the LBSCR west coast line at Dyke junction, adjacent to the present Aldrington, to the terminus 3½ miles away (Fig 10). In this distance the line climbed through over 400ft with continuous reverse curvature and a ruling gradient of 1 in 40/41. The Dyke station was still a quarter of a mile away from the summit of the Downs, and there were another 200ft to climb on foot to reach this vantage point. Even with the advantage of access by rail, the Dyke remained bare of residences, although an hotel and funfair were built. There were no intermediate stopping places until Rowan Halt was opened half a mile beyond the junction with the coast line on 18 December 1933. At the same period a private halt was opened three-quarters of a mile short of the Dyke terminus to serve the nearby golf club.

Top left: **The isolated station at The Dyke.** *Madgwick Collection/IAL*

Above left: **The Dyke branch winds its way through a chalk cutting on the steep descent to sea level.** *Madgwick Collection/IAL*

Above: **One 'balloon' coach and 'E4' 0-6-2T No 2505 form the Dyke branch train leaving Brighton in 1937.** *E. R. Wethersett*

Fig 10. Brighton branches and halts. The word 'halt' has now been dropped from former halts remaining open, and Portslade has lost 'West Hove'.

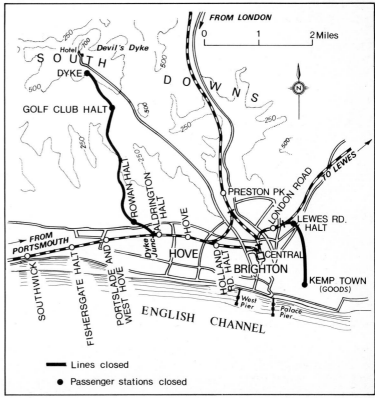

The line was worked by the LBSC from the outset. When Marsh's 'motors' were introduced on the west coast line in 1905 a halt was opened on that line at the junction with the Dyke branch, and was named Dyke Junction Halt (later changed to Aldrington), and there was another stopping place for Dyke trains at Holland Road on the coast line in Hove, approximately on the site of the original Hove station. Before the 'motors', tank engines worked the Dyke trains, running round at the terminus and returning bunker-first (there was no turntable). After the opening of Rowan Halt about half the branch services in winter terminated there; the halt served a rapidly developing housing estate. By that time the private car and the motorbus were carrying most of the Dyke tourist traffic. Trains running through to the terminus normally consisted of one 'Balloon' centre-gangway coach and motive power was often a Billington 'E4' class 0-6-2 tank. A Sentinel-Cammell steam railcar started work on the line in 1932 and remained for two years before being transferred to the Dunton Green-Westerham branch in Kent.

For some time the powers at Waterloo had looked askance at this miniature mountain railway with its diminishing traffic prospects. At last they decided it must go, naming 31 December 1938 as the final day. In his book on secondary and branch lines in Southern England* Edwin Course contrasted the lengthy treatment accorded by the local press to the Dyke branch when it opened with the somewhat bald announcement of its

*Edwin Course, *Railways of Southern England: Secondary and Branch Lines*, Batsford, 1974.

closure. A more graphic account of this melancholy occasion was given by a contributor to *The Railway Magazine* of March 1939, who had ridden on the last train:

'The signalman extinguished the oil lamp in his little cabin, emerged from the darkness and locked the door behind him. Once more all clambered aboard, once more No 2505 lifted up her voice, and the train moved away. Another volley of detonators burst upon the night. Those who looked back saw only the Downs looming against the starless sky, their dark masses unbroken by any gleam of light shining cosily from the tiny station . . . As we approached Brighton pandemonium again broke loose, aided and abetted as before by the loco yard and the shed staff. At last, when "Journey's End" had indeed been reached, an improvised band struck up the inevitable "Auld Lang Syne" and other ditties of a fare-thee-well nature, while many who were not helping to swell the shindy gambolled gleefully upon the platform. But the real railway lovers disappeared from the scene, feeling that all this hullabaloo struck a discordant note. The Old Year was dying; the Dyke branch was dead.'

The above passage reflects an early reaction to a ceremonial that was to become increasingly familiar after World War 2, but steam itself, not simply unremunerative services, was to be threatened. When I visited Brighton shed (Fig 11) in 1947, however, that cloud was still on the distant horizon. Brighton was providing two main line engines daily for the cross-country trains to Bournemouth and Cardiff. The Plymouth train was usually worked by a Salisbury engine, and at that time a Salisbury 'West Country' Pacific brought it into Brighton every night. On Saturday, however, Brighton might have to find power for three cross-countries, calling on its 'Schools', a 'B4X' and a Maunsell Mogul. On these occasions the Brighton engine on the Plymouth train worked to and from Salisbury, as was the usual practice on the Cardiff service. Stroudley 'D' tanks shared stopping services on the west coast line with Billinton radials, large and small.

There were five through engine workings to London daily by the routes east of the main line. That from Culver junction via Horsted Keynes to East Grinstead was called the 'Inner Circle', while the route via Uckfield and Eridge was the 'Outer Circle'. Some Outer Circle trains conveyed through portions for London and for Tunbridge Wells, the latter being handed over at Eridge to a train that had come from Eastbourne, in exchange for Oxted line carriages off the Eastbourne train. These were hardy survivors of the workings inaugurated with the opening of the Ashurst spur recorded earlier in this chapter.

Through trains between London and Brighton via Horsham could by this time be regarded as an extinct

Left: **The Sentinel steam railcar which worked on the Dyke branch between 1932 and 1934.** *IAL*

Fig 11. **Brighton mpd in the last years of steam.**

species. In 1952 there was still an 05.05 from London Bridge, travelling to Horsham via Sutton and Dorking, which made 27 stops on the way to the coast and took 3hr 19min. There was no through service in the opposite direction. It was an oddity that could not survive. For many years the official thinking seemed to be that if you lived in the area between Sutton and Dorking you went to Bognor and liked it. Brighton was not for you.

Main line steam workings to and from Brighton in the late 1940 and 1950s were principally van trains, although passengers prepared to catch the 03.25 newspaper train from London Bridge could still enjoy a steam-hauled journey down the main line. The train ran to Eastbourne via Brighton and conveyed third class passengers. Brighton shed powered the 18.12 and 23.28 van trains to London Bridge, which called at Haywards Heath to pick up vehicles from the east coast line, and at Three Bridges for those from west of Angmering and the Mid-Sussex line. Billinton Moguls, the 'B4X' class, Marsh tanks or an 'L1' 4-4-0 of Eastern Section origin were the usual engines for these duties. The shed in 1947 housed some 40 engines in all. Wainwright 4-4-0s on through trains from Tonbridge were frequent visitors, and a Tonbridge-based 'H' class 0-4-04T on Tonbridge-Brighton turns often filled in with a Brighton-Horsham and return working between its trips. Often to be seen on shed was an Eastern Section 'P' class 0-6-0 tank based at Brighton for shunting at Kingston Wharf but the sidings there were closed in 1968.

The van trains which kept Brighton locomotives busy in the last days of steam continued into the age of the

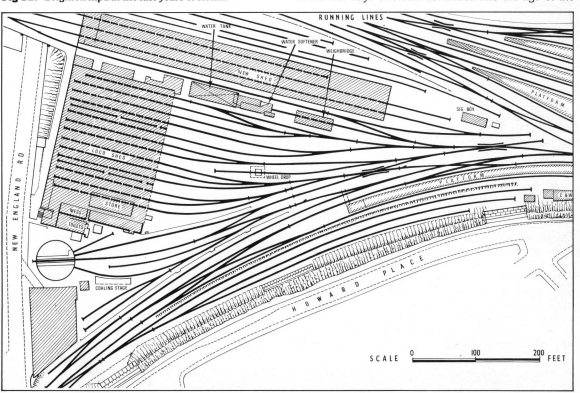

Engines at Brighton mpd in 1947: *(Top left)* R. J. Billinton's 'C2' 0-6-0 goods engine rebuilt as a 'C2X'. This operation was carried out on No 2539 by the Southern Railway, although the process had been begun by Marsh; *(Centre left)* Billinton's Class E5 0-6-2T No 2405, originally named *Fernhurst*. The class had 5ft 6in wheels as against the 5ft wheels of the ubiquitous Class E4s; *(Bottom left)* No 2073 was one of the 'B4s' built by Sharp, Stewart and was named *Westminster*. It was rebuilt as a 'B4X' in 1923. *All Author*

Above: 4SUB unit No 4699 makes an unusual appearance on the west coast line on 4 January 1969, forming a Portsmouth-Brighton stopping train. *Rodney E. Smith*

diesel and the electro-diesel. This traffic was still flourishing in 1980, when the parcels area served by Brighton extended to Chichester in the west and Lewes in the east. Van trains were made up in the Upper Yard, some running to Bricklayers Arms with London traffic, and some with vans for other Regions and the North to Clapham Junction. Vans for Kentish destinations and the Guildford/Reading area and beyond were detached at Redhill. A shadow was cast on these activities in the autumn of 1980 when British Rail announced its intention to withdraw its parcels collection and delivery service in June of the following year.

Most investors in the London & Brighton Railway probably looked for a return from passenger traffic, but

freight formed a useful background, less subject to fluctuations, and its transport by rail was a valuable service to Sussex towns and villages. As described in Chapter 1 the original connection to the Brighton goods station was from the Shoreham branch. This was an awkward arrangement after the opening of the London line, for a goods train from London had to run into Brighton station, back out on to the Shoreham line, and then proceed over the junction to the goods station.

The situation was improved in the early 1850s by building a new line to the goods yard from the London main line (see Fig 2, Chapter 2). It diverged on the east side about half a mile outside the terminus and descended a gradient of 1 in 53 to pass under the east coast line just on the Brighton side of the London Road viaduct. Still descending, for as has been seen in Chapter 1 the goods station was 30ft lower than the passenger station, the line crossed the New England Road on its own bridge, a short distance from the bridge carrying the main lines, and so entered the goods yard. When the new line was ready the tunnel connection from the Shoreham line was abandoned. The tunnel still exists. It served as a dug-out for a telecommunications centre in World War 2 and has since been used as a rifle range, its original purpose long forgotten.

The junction of the goods line with the main line was near the 50th milepost. Lovers Walk signalbox controlled entry to the reception and sorting sidings at this point. These sidings became known as the Upper Yard, while the yard at the goods station was the Lower Yard (Fig 12). Movements in the Upper Yard and to and from the

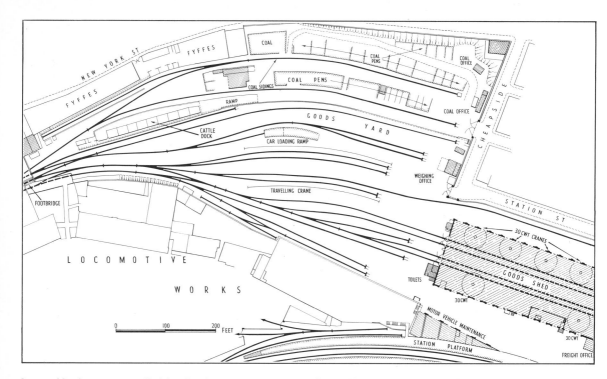

Lower Yard were controlled by Brighton Upper Goods box. The LBSC goods depot in London was Willow Walk, which made it seem that the Brighton sidings *ought* to be called Lovers Walk. But Lovers Walk sidings were the rolling stock sidings on the up side of the main line and disclaimed all connection with the goods establishment opposite. The author of an article in *Transport & Travel Monthly* of September 1912 who gave the title 'From Willow Walk to Lovers Walk' to his account of a trip with a goods train from London to Brighton was correct in so far that his train was shunted into the yard from Lovers Walk box, but the heading may have misled later generations.

Although an improvement on the original arrangement, the final layout of goods lines at Brighton had drawbacks. Trains for the east coast and west coast lines from the Upper Yard could not reach them without reversal. A line called the Hastings Siding extended from the yard to the station approaches independently of the passenger tracks. An eastbound train would be propelled out of the yard along this siding until the locomotive had passed Montpelier junction. It would then stop and move forward over the junction on to the east coast line. In accomplishing this manoeuvre the 'tail' of the train would probably have to be backed into Platform 10, or the bay No 11 if this was not occupied by the Kemp Town train, so that the locomotive could clear the Montpelier junction points. Trains leaving the Upper Yard for the west coast line could be propelled to sidings at Preston Park, crossing the main lines in the process, and then run forward over the Cliftonville Curve. Wagons from the west coast line for London could be worked to the Preston Park sidings and attached to northbound trains

there. West coast line traffic was also attached and detached in sidings at Hassocks.

Exchange of wagons at Hassocks took place on the freight train trip described by the writer of the article 'From Willow Walk to Lovers Walk' mentioned above. His train was the 07.40 mixed freight with '50 on', 18 of the wagons being for Hassocks. They had left Willow Walk with about 2,600 gallons in the tanks, but by Hassocks the supply was almost exhausted and after coming to a halt the engine ran forward to the water column to replenish before backing on to the train again to detach the 18 wagons and pick up others. The author continued:

'Preston Park station is soon reached, just after which we cross over on to the local line and soon are passing the sidings, which are filled with railway wagons and coaches in every stage of dilapidation and repair. All signals being "off" we continue slowly past Lovers Walk signalbox until the fireman, who has been looking back, sings out "Over!" This signifies that he has received a signal from the guard that we are over the points leading to the sidings. We stop just beneath Montpelier junction signals and soon receive another hand signal to shunt back into the sidings, where the train, after it has been secured with sprags placed in the spokes of the wheels and with the side brakes is to be left in the care of the shunters, number takers, wagon examiners and greasers.'

The movement of wagons between the Upper and Lower Yards was the subject of special regulations in the Appendix to the working timetable. A special incline brake was provided and with this vehicle the load was not

Fig 12. 'Lower Yard' and the goods station buildings.

Below: **Class H2 Atlantic No 32421, *North Foreland,* takes the 17.30 parcels train to London Bridge out of Brighton on 4 July 1951.** *P. Lynch*

to exceed 35 mixed wagons coming up the grade and 40 loaded wagons going down. The special brake had to be the leading vehicle going down, and the rear vehicle coming up. With over 20 wagons going down, one sprag had to be used for every 10 wagons or part of 10. Four sprags had always to be carried in the incline brake.

When any brake vehicle other than the special brake was in use, it had to be at the leading end of a train being propelled from the Upper to the Lower Yard, and a guard or shunter must ride in it. The load going down in these circumstances was restricted to 20 vehicles, and one sprag was to be used when over 10 vehicles. A train

might be drawn down the incline into the Lower Yard and need then not have a brake at the rear, but must not exceed 20 vehicles, and one sprag must be used when over 15. A train coming up the grade must have a brake van at the rear, with a guard or shunter on board, and if it was not the special incline brake the load was not to exceed 20 vehicles.

The 7.40pm Willow Walk-Brighton was still running in 1921. At that time it conveyed wagons for Brighton, Kemp Town, Falmer, Hove and west coast line stations to Angmering. The Hove and west coast portion was marshalled next to the engine for dropping at Hassocks as already described, and the working timetable showed a departure from Hassocks for Worthing and Angmering at 4.00am. A 3.00am from Brighton to Lewes conveyed wagons for east coast line stations, and at 3.25 a freight left for Havant, calling at Worthing and Ford Junction to attach and detach wagons. There was an important up service from Brighton to Willow Walk at 12.15am, calling

Left: **'K' class Mogul No 32346 enters Shoreham-by-Sea with a Bristol-Brighton through train in April 1960.** *John C. Baker*

Bottom left: **Behind Class 73/1 electro-diesel No 73.127 at Three Bridges on 1 September 1975 are vans from Bricklayers Arms for Brighton, Eastbourne, Horsham and Chichester.** *John Scrace*

Below: **A diesel shunter marshals vans in the dock between Platforms 7 and 8 at Brighton while the 17.45 'Brighton Belle' awaits departure on 5 September 1968.** *John Scrace*

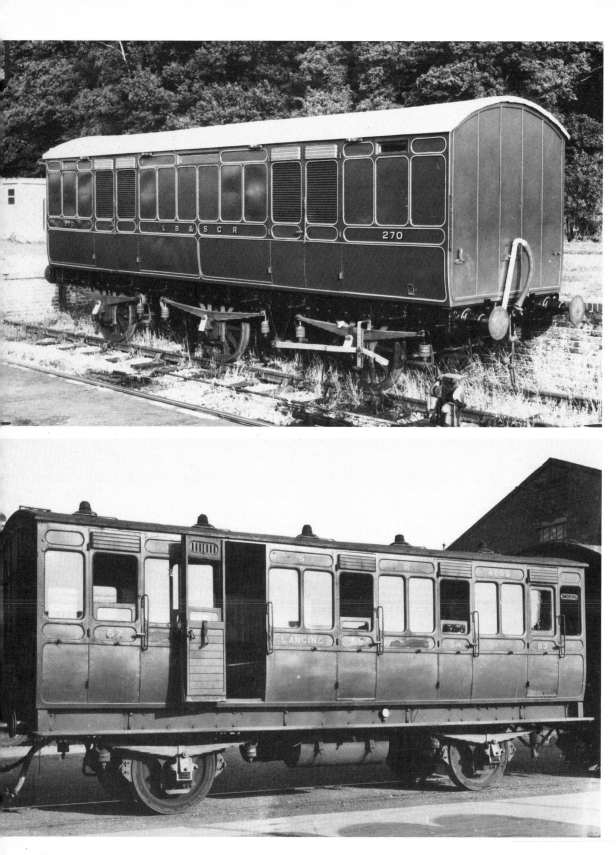

Left: An LBSC milk van of about 1908 restored and preserved on the Bluebell Railway at Horsted Keynes. *R. C. Riley*

Below left: A glimpse of LBSC third class austerity which survived to carry Southern Railway insignia. *Madgwick Collection/IAL*

Below: Many workers at the Lancing carriage and wagon works lived in Brighton. Their daily special train – the 'Lancing Belle' – passes Aldrington on 10 April 1956 with 'E4' 0-6-2T No 32511 at the head. *W. M. J. Jackson*

Bottom: The first wagon built at Lancing Works, photographed on 13 April 1909. *Madgwick Collection/IAL*

Left: **An LBSC four-wheel van.**
Madgwick Collection/IAL

Centre left: **Six-wheel goods brake.**
Madgwick Collection/IAL

Below: **A four-wheel goods brake in use as a departmental vehicle at Three Bridges in 1967.** *John Scrace*

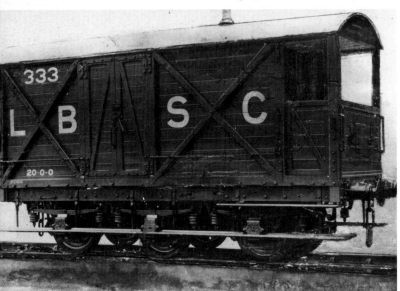

Top: The old Lovers Walk signalbox is about to be demolished, replaced by the new box alongside. Locomotive No 378 on the right is one of the 2-4-0 'Crystal Palace' well tanks built by Craven at Brighton in 1958/9 for the West End of London & Crystal Palace Railway, which eventually gave the LBSC access to Victoria. In this picture it has been rebuilt as a side tank. *Bucknall Collection/IAL*

Above: **Montpelier Junction, Brighton, with a Tonbridge train taking the east coast line on the right and the main line continuing past wagons in the Upper Yard.** *G. Daniels*

at Three Bridges and Norwood Junction. Wagons for all stations on the Midhurst and Tunbridge Wells lines were detached at Three Bridges.

Lillie Bridge on the West London Extension line was another London destination of freight services from Brighton. In the LBSC peak years before the First World War there were trains at 6.30pm and 9.00pm, the latter calling at Preston Park to attach wagons. Hove also made up through freight trains to London, sending services to Battersea Yard and Willow Walk. There were various local trips from Brighton to Hove, Hassocks, Shoreham and Horsham, including one to Three Bridges via Shoreham and Horsham. Eastwards from Brighton freight was worked over the secondary routes to East Grinstead and Tunbridge Wells as well as along the coast line, where there were fast services at 2.00am to Hastings, 8.15am to St Leonards, and 12.35pm to Bexhill.

Writers and artists have done little to preserve the Brighton line's freight image as compared with their efforts on behalf of the 'Southern Belle' and the 'City Limited'. One must try to recreate it mentally by nodding over old working timetables in the somnolence of a public library reading room. Then, perhaps, a dream will come of the 2.00am Brighton-Hastings pounding along on its non-stop run to Polegate. It if had less than '30 on' it would stop at Lewes East Junction to attach important wagons, but with its van carrying Hastings mail this was an aristocrat among freight trains and clearly not to be hailed for pick-up duties without good reason. And that occasional stamping and snorting? Does it proceed from our fellow readers? Or are they the sounds, deadened by the passage of many years, of impatient cattle in their wagons on the Hove-Willow Walk train that called at Norwood Junction if it had cattle traffic for the northern

lines to detach? Those bald timetable comments and footnotes can be powerfully evocative.

In the 1960s British Rail's policy of promoting long-distance freight transport by fast trains led to various services receiving names. Brighton shared in the glamourising when a new Southern Region freight timetable based on diesel-electric traction was introduced in 1964. From 6 January in that year a train called the 'Midlands Merseyman' left Brighton at 15.30 with freight for Stoke-on-Trent, Manchester, Warrington and Liverpool. Goods could be loaded at Brighton up to 14.00. The train then called at East Croydon, where goods were accepted up to 15.30. The next stop was Willesden, where the Class 33 diesel which had worked through from Brighton came off and was replaced by an LMR diesel. This direct link to the LMR, avoiding Norwood Yard, enabled overnight delivery to be offered for most of the freight. A similar service, the 'North East Trader', followed in November 1965, serving 15 industrial centres in the north-east. But a new era in rail freight transport was approaching, in which the emphasis was to be on serving customers forwarding full wagonloads, or complete trainloads. If in the future Brighton industry generates the right kind of traffic the activity of the Upper Yard could yet revive.

Below: **Brighton Upper Goods signalbox.** *John Scrace*

Right: '**K' class Mogul No 341, with top feed, heads a down freight near Hassocks.** *Bucknall Collection/IAL*

Below right: **A Hove-Three Bridges freight via Shoreham is headed by 'C2x' 0-6-0 No 32534 near Horsham on 13 June 1969.** *John Scrace*

Above: **A west coast line freight with 'K' class Mogul No 32337 in charge stands on the goods loop at Hove on 26 September 1961.** *D. H. Sawyer*

Left: **Brighton goods yard after closure in 1980.** *Author*

7. Brighton in the 1980s

Brighton today remains a railway centre as well as a railway terminus. There was a time in the early 1970s when the future of the east and west coast coastal services seemed in doubt but a vigorous promotion campaign was launched in May 1972 to remind the public of their usefulness. In a style appropriate to a seaside resort, a 'Miss Coastway' was chosen from local talent and crowned at a 'Coastway Dance' in Brighton, since when the two services have been known as 'Coastway East' and 'Coastway West.' There was also a competition with a prize of £100 for the most convincing list of six reasons why the community would continue to need local railway services. On a more mundane plane, timetables were adjusted to improve connections between the two routes. Today the trains are well patronised. The east to west coastal road through Brighton is common with the sea front from the Palace Pier to the western end of Hove, and negotiating it by car in the summer can be a testing experience rather than a pleasure.

With 400 trains in 24 hours, Brighton is among the busiest stations in the BR passenger network. Platforms are numbered 1 to 9 from west to east. Normally west coast trains use Platforms 1 and 2, Platforms 3 and 7 are for main line services, and Platform 9 for the east coast line. There is a wide carriage road between Platforms 7 and 8, where parcels traffic can be handled. Two sidings terminate in a dock at the northern end of the carriage road (Fig 13).

The 'middle siding' between Platforms 2 and 3 is a reminder of steam days, and of the closeness of the shed to the station platforms, for locomotives coming off shed

Fig 13. Diagram of Brighton platforms and approaches (1980).

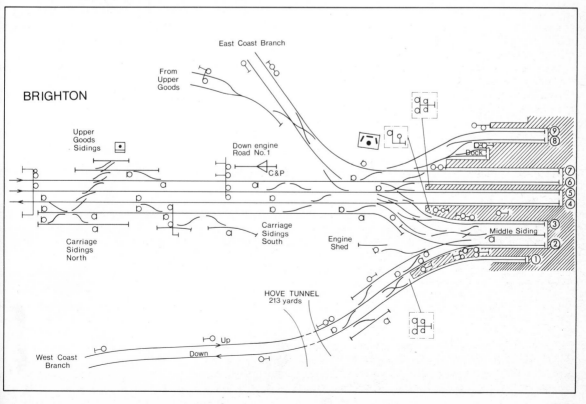

had to run into the siding before they could be despatched to their various duties. The 'middle siding' is still used today for movements of diesel and electro-diesel locomotives and connects with a siding on a corner of the old steam depot site where they can be stabled.

In normal working east coast and west coast trains keep to their own sides of the station. The connection between the two routes via Platform 3 still has its limitations. The crossover giving access from the platform to the west coast line is so close to the buffer stops that only a 4-car set can leave by it. In LBSC days there were some through trains and through coaches between the two coastal lines (Chapter 3). There are no regular workings of this kind today, although football specials sometimes run through from the east coast line to Hove, which is the nearest station to the Brighton ground. They can do so by taking the main line to Preston Park and reversing there to take the Cliftonville Curve. The exit from Platform 3 to the west coast line has been used regularly, however, by an early morning service worked by a 4-car set which stands at the buffers while the country end of the platform, clear of the crossover, is occupied by a train for the main line. Platform 2 also has a connection to the main line that can be used by short trains.

When approaching Brighton station from Queens Road, parts of Mocatta's original station house can still be seen above the awning over the forecourt; some of the present administrative offices are in parts of the old building. The responsibilities of the Area Manager at

Above: **Class 414 (2HAP) emu No 6019 heads the 09.10 Brighton to Portsmouth Harbour semi-fast in Platform 2 at Brighton on 7 June 1980. Platform 3 and the crossover to the west coast line are on the left; 'middle siding' in centre.** *Brian Bennett.*

Above right: **The entrance for vehicles.** *British Rail*

Right: **The arches of Mocatta's colonnades are still echoed in the present-day entrance for passengers.** *British Rail*

Brighton extend to Shoreham in the west, Burgess Hill on the main line, and Bexhill in the east. Although Mocatta's colonnades have gone, they are echoed in the arched windows and doorways of the present frontage, which has been generally tidied and much improved visually in recent years. In December 1979 a new travel centre was opened, followed in August 1980 by a new ticket office. Both these important points of contact between the public and the railway are attractively styled. In the travel centre the counter is shaped to provide individual bays for those making enquiries, heightening the impression of personal service, while in the ticket office small ticket windows have given place to all-glass screens with stainless steel surrounds. Another improvement here was the separation of the ticket hall from the entrance foyer. Previously the windows were in one side of the foyer itself and passengers booked their tickets amid the general flow of traffic to and from the concourse.

At the time of writing the concourse is still dominated by a departure indicator with each column of station names headed by a conventional clock face set to show when the next train leaves; and as yet the large clock suspended over the concourse has not gone digital. There are refreshments in the cafeteria and bar near Platform 1, and a trolley service in the concourse caters for the traveller in a hurry. In Fig 14 the station is shown in relation to the principal thoroughfares of modern Brighton.

With the demolition of the locomotive works and the opening of a car park on the site, the public has become familiar with a view of Brighton station which was previously hidden. Although Terminus Road climbs steeply along the curve of the west coast line, little of the station can be seen from it but the roof. A high wall has frustrated generations of train spotters. In contrast the car park on the opposite side of the railway is at platform level and from here the whole impressive extent of the building and its overall roof is visible. This view emphasises the difference in width between the two main roof spans and the narrower third span over the east coast platforms – a difference less evident from inside the station. A length of platform awning still in situ on the eastern outside wall in 1980 was a memorial to the old Platform 10, little used since the withdrawal of the Kemp Town branch passenger service before the war and removed in 1971 when the car park was built.

Among the constant flow of passengers through Brighton station every day, probably only a small proportion were aware of the goods station alongside it on the east side but at a lower level. In recent years it has been an NCL (National Carriers) depot, but a few wagons carrying miscellaneous consignments continued to be handled until this business was terminated in October 1980. At the same time the connection to the Lower Yard at the goods station to the Upper Yard was padlocked out of use. This again was an aspect of Brighton railway geography little in evidence to the visitor or even the resident until the car park was built and the approach road was carried across the cutting in which the line descended to the goods station. Some will remember it, however, from the days when steam locomotives stored at Brighton were on view in the station and passenger trips were run over the goods line with a diesel shunter hauling a single coach.

Right: **The ticket hall. Before this improvement in 1980 the ticket windows were in the entrance foyer.** *British Rail*

Below right: **The main roof spans seen from the roadway between Platforms 7 and 8.**

Fig 14. Lines in Brighton today in relation to the principal thoroughfares. The course of the Kemp Town branch (closed) is shown dotted; to avoid confusion the Cliftonville curve (Preston Park to Hove) is shown solid, although partly in tunnel.

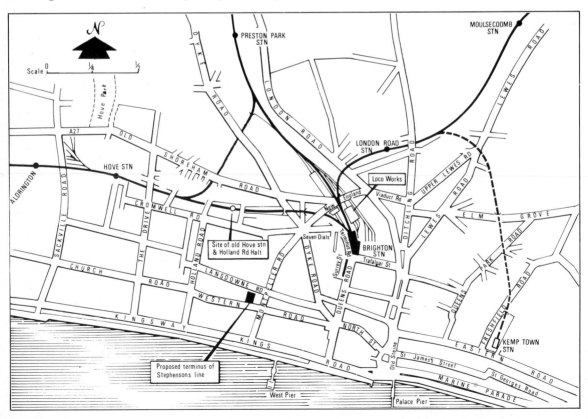

Contemporary conditions impose utility rather than elegance in station design, as demonstrated at Aldrington *(Above)* **and Fishersgate** *(Right)* **The electro-diesel trundling mineral wagons past Fishersgate is No 73.133.** *British Rail/John G. Glover*

Although wagonload traffic to Brighton was discontinued, trainload traffic continued to pass through the area – coal to the coal concentration depot at Hove; oil from Fawley to Salfords, the fuel storage depot for Gatwick Airport; and occasional stone traffic to West Worthing. Trains running between the west coast line and the main line took the Cliftonville Curve and sometimes changed locomotives at Hove.

The Red Star parcels service by scheduled passenger trains has proved increasingly popular with the business world and the general public. A new and more conveniently situated Red Star office was among the improvements at Brighton station in the late 1970s.

Considerable revision of passenger services on the Central Division of the Southern Region took place in 1978, based on studies of population growth, shifting centres of business activity and changing patterns of travel. The development of Croydon as a business and shopping centre led to the decision to stop all trains there, and so from the May 1978 timetable the long traditional 'Brighton non-stop' became a thing of the past. With one stop at East Croydon, however, the corresponding off-peak hourly buffet car trains to and from Victoria were still publicly scheduled to make the journey in two or three minutes under the hour. Semi-fasts made more stops south of Haywards Heath to cater for expanding residential areas north of Brighton but omitted their previous stops at Clapham Junction and Redhill. They included buffet cars for the first time. The down trains stopped at Gatwick to pick up only, and the up trains to set down.

Some 6½ per cent of the air traffic through Gatwick using the railway comes from south of the airport. Gatwick, indeed, was one of the major traffic influences considered in planning the new timetables. A major traffic flow is to and from Portsmouth and West Sussex towns served by the Victoria-Portsmouth trains, which were diverted from the Sutton/Dorking route to travel via Three Bridges, calling at Gatwick. Stops at Gatwick were inserted in the schedules of the hourly trains between Victoria and Littlehampton via Hove, giving the populous residential area immediately west of Brighton the convenience of a through service for air travellers. 'I had a gentleman for Australia first thing this morning', a member of the staff at Hove station was overheard to say recently, and his words were very symptomatic of the Brighton line today.

The new timetables concentrated London-Brighton stopping services on Victoria, accelerating them by some 10min by omitting some stops north of Gatwick. The London Bridge stopping service on the Brighton line was terminated at Three Bridges with a good connection there for all stations south.

Peak hours saw extra trains and changed service patterns. The proportions of business traffic from Brighton to Victoria and London Bridge have

approximately reversed since earlier years, Victoria now taking 60 per cent and London Bridge 40 per cent. Business in London has spread westward, and the usefulness of Victoria to commuters has been much increased by London Transport's Victoria Line. Only minor changes were made to the new timetables up to 1980. Among them was the insertion of stops at Clapham Junction by some peak hour trains which did not originally call there, to provide for the growing interchange traffic with South-Western Division trains at that point.

No close equivalent to the 'City Limited' remained in 1980. The fastest train from Brighton to London Bridge was the 07.32, doing the journey in 61min with stops at Preston Park, Burgess Hill and East Croydon only, but it is doubtful whether the patrons of the 'Limited' in its heyday would have contemplated starting their journey to the City at such an hour. Other peak hour trains to London Bridge in the 1980 service originated at Littlehampton or West Worthing, calling at Hove and then serving Brighton's residential hinterland with stops at Preston Park, Hassocks, and Burgess Hill. The London Bridge traffic is very much associated with commuters employed in the banking and other establishments of the City's 'Square Mile'. They are outnumbered today by those bound for the offices of enterprises of which not only were the names unknown but often the activities were undreamed of when the first business trains steamed out of Brighton.

A year after the timetable changes of 1978, through trains between Manchester and Brighton returned. Gatwick Airport was their primary target, but extension to

Brighton was operationally convenient and also revealed a useful business traffic potential for through services between Brighton, the Midlands and the North. The trains were routed via Clapham Junction and the West London line, but instead of following the 'Sunny South' itinerary to Willesden they diverged at North Pole junction, Acton, on to the Western Region, continuing via Reading and Oxford to Birmingham. Also in 1979 a seasonal Saturdays only through service was put on between Brighton and Bristol via the west coast line, Southampton, Salisbury, and Bath, giving connections for South Wales and other points in the West at Bristol. A completely new cross-country service was introduced in 1980 when through trains began running hourly between Reading, Redhill and Gatwick Airport. Once again a facility introduced primarily as a rail/air link was not only well patronised in that respect but brought a useful bonus of other traffic. With frequent trains from Brighton to Gatwick, travellers found the service convenient for journeys to the Reading/Guildford area and more attractive than the alternative of changing at Redhill into the all-stations Redhill-Reading trains. The cross-country offer from Brighton was completed by the long-established Brighton-Exeter through service, which still ran on Saturdays only but operated all the year round. In the 1981 timetables the Brighton-Bristol service was retimed, extended to Cardiff, and scheduled to run on Saturdays throughout the year. A new service from Brighton was shown on Sundays, running to Bristol westbound and starting from Cardiff eastbound.

An encouraging sign of the importance attached by the public to purely local train services was the opening in

May 1980 of a new station on the east coast line at Moulsecoomb, 1¾ miles from Brighton. This was a response to pressure for better travel facilities for the adjacent Brighton Polytechnic and the Hollingdean housing estate. All Coastway East services stopped there, giving the new station a service at 20min intervals in each direction in off-peak hours, with extra trains in the peaks. The two platforms at Moulsecoomb are linked by a footbridge, with a waiting room, ticket office and staff accommodation on the up (to Brighton) side and a waiting shelter on the other. This was the first completely new station built by the Southern Region since Southampton Airport in 1966.

Coastway East trains from Brighton in 1980 ran in sequence to Eastbourne, Hastings and Ore; to Eastbourne, and to Seaford. The Ore train did not stop at Berwick or Glynde, but the others called at all stations. Coastway West similarly had three trains an hour from Brighton: semi-fast to Portsmouth Harbour, all stations (except Hilsea) to Portsmouth Harbour; and all stations to Littlehampton. At Hove there was also the hourly fast train from Victoria, calling at Shoreham-by-Sea, Worthing and stations to Littlehampton. On both coastal routes the inwards services to Brighton were similar to those just mentioned. Hove station layout is shown in Fig 15.

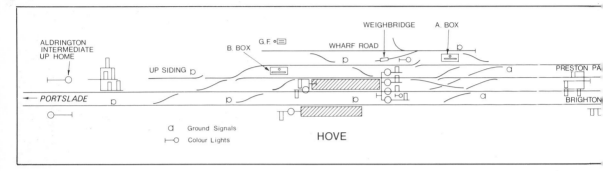

Fig 15. Running lines and signals at Hove in the 1970s.

Right: An arrival from Coastway East passes Brighton signalbox, perched on all that remains of the works buildings. The works site has been cleared and the car park is in course of development. *G. W. Morrison*

Below: The platforms and passenger entrance at Moulsecoomb station, opened to serve the eastern end of Brighton, beyond London Road, in 1980. *Both Author*

Top: **The 08.30 (Saturdays) from Brighton to Bristol gathers speed as it passes through Hove on 7 June 1980.** *B. Bennett*

Above: **One of the coaches that ferried passengers between the station and the marina terminal of the jetfoil service to Dieppe.** *Southdown Motor Services*

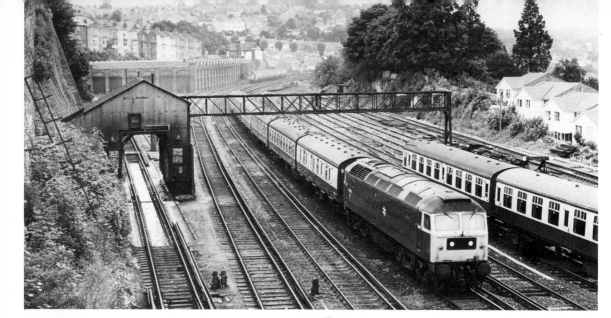

Above: **Successor to the 'Sunny South Special': No 47.482 passes the Lovers Walk carriage washing plant as it approaches Brighton with the 07.44 from Manchester Piccadilly. The old Pullman Works are in the background.** *Les Bertram*

Left: **Nos 33.001 and 33.033 double-head the Brighton-Exeter through train on the banks of the River Hamble at Bursledon.** *John Scrace*

Below: **Electro-diesel No 71.133 marshals empty mineral wagons in the sidings at Hove, which now serve a coal concentration depot, the former general goods depot being closed.** *John G. Glover*

In recent years a 'hypermarket' in Dieppe and Brighton's large multiple stores have attracted visitors on shopping trips from opposite sides of the Channel, to the extent, it is said, that an Englishman in one Brighton store on a summer Saturday, may well feel that he belongs to a minority group. Sealink excursions by the Newhaven-Dieppe ferries have brought extra traffic to the Brighton-Seaford trains. Until September 1980 the operator of a jetfoil service between Brighton Marina and Dieppe provided motorcoach transport from Brighton station to the Marina, but as the company also put on a through road service from London the extra traffic by rail was small. When visitors from Dieppe used the coach for returning to the Marina after their day in Brighton and made the station their rendezvous, the accumulation of non-fare-paying travellers in busy periods could be an embarrassment to the station staff. The jetfoil service was suspended indefinitely after disruption caused by the French trawlermen's strike in August 1980 and other problems.

The establishment of the maintenance depot for electric rolling stock at Brighton when the main line was electrified has been recorded in Chapter 5. Immediately north of the depot are the Lovers Walk carriage sidings, a name still recalling in this built-up area a footpath which once rambled in romantic seclusion to Preston church. There is still a Lovers Walk in Brighton, but now it is only a close between Preston Road and Dyke Road Drive on the east side of the railway opposite the sidings. From Stanford Road, above the sidings on the west, the tower of Preston church can be seen among distant trees. An early guide to the London & Brighton Railway remarked that 'the church is a pleasant termination to the "lovers' walk", which here leads to it'.

At the time of writing Brighton Inspection Shed is responsible for all Central Division main line stock. Emu stock is examined for mechanical fitness for service every 24 hours, wherever it may be, and minor repairs or adjustments are carried out before it is passed for traffic. Some 75 units a day are examined in the shed and Lovers Walk sidings, while in addition units at Preston Park, Montpelier sidings, and in the station are examined by the Area Maintenance Engineer's staff. Trains are cleaned, marshalled and formed ready for service at Lovers Walk. After internal cleaning, stock passes through a carriage washing plant.

For the more detailed examination at monthly intervals units are brought into the maintenance shed. At this stage some electrical items come into the schedule. Line contactors (corresponding to 'mains switches' between the supply and the traction equipment) are checked for burned contacts or other faults. Contact tips are replaced if necessary but in the event of a more serious defect the whole contactor is changed. Shoegear is examined for wear of the slippers which collect current from the live rail, and their height when off the live rail is checked. If they hang too low they are liable to damage when meeting the end of a live rail after a gap. The rail ends are ramped, and correctly adjusted shoes lift and slide on to them without trouble. The motor-generators which provide a 70V supply for control circuits and lighting are also checked at these four-weekly inspections, and compressor oil levels are verified. Among other items in the maintenance schedule at this stage are window wipers, route indicators, cab and instrument lights, and a heater test.

A more detailed examination of electrical equipment takes place in maintenance periods occurring at intervals of between three and six months. At this stage traction motors and control gear in the underframe equipment cases are checked. Motor brushgear and commutators are accessible for examination through inspection covers without lifting the coach bodies, and brushes are changed if necessary.

After completing the maintenance cycle at Brighton, units are sent to one of the Regional repair depots where a general overhaul of running gear is carried out. This occurs at intervals ranging between 10 and 20 months, mileage being taken into account as well as time. Every three to four years units go to a British Rail Engineering works for a general overhaul of brake gear and bodywork.

No locomotives are based at Brighton, the electro-diesels being allocated to Stewarts Lane, and the Class 33 diesels to Hither Green and Eastleigh. Both types are regular visitors, and since 1979 have been joined by Class 47 diesels working through from Birmingham on the Manchester-Brighton trains. A refuelling plant in the maintenance depot dispenses some 1,700gal of fuel oil in a week. Locomotives are due for a service check every three days. Maintenance Control at Croydon notifies Brighton if a visiting locomotive is due for this procedure, and the Brighton staff carry it out.

The depot, with a staff of over 100, works round the clock. Apart from the maintenance shown to be necessary at the various inspections, renewal of brake blocks goes on continuously, night and day. A 4-coach unit has a total of 64 cast iron brake blocks, each block usually weighing 21lb; a new block will need replacing after approximately three weeks in service, resulting in an average weekly usage of blocks at the depot of nearly 4,000. Light repairs to units are carried out as required, not only at the regular examinations. They are often necessary as first aid after vandalism. Approximately 3,600sq ft of seating materials are used each year in repairing torn seats. Other vulnerable items are ashtrays (600 replaced a year), curtains (1,300 replaced), windows (800 replaced) and lamps, of which 150,000 need replacement every year.

Depot staff are on call to deal with breakdowns or derailments over a wide area which extends to Earlswood on the main line, Fishbourne Crossing (near Chichester) on the west coast line, and St Leonards on the east coast line; also included are Wivelsfield to Lewes and Seaford; Three Bridges to Horsham, and from south of Dorking, via Horsham, to Bognor and Littlehampton. A 45ton steam crane and a road lorry with power jacking equipment are stationed at the depot for dealing with derailments.

In 1968 a combined engineering depot for the

Brighton area was opened on the site of the old steam shed, immediately south of the rolling stock maintenance depot. Here are stationed staff of the Civil Engineer, the Signal & Telecommunications Engineer, and the Outdoor Machinery Section of the Chief Mechanical & Electrical Engineer's Department. One section of the depot maintains NCL road vehicles under an agreement made between BR and National Carriers Limited when the latter was formed. On the same site the British Railways Board has the Ultrasonic Equipment Maintenance Section where the repair and servicing of non-destructive testing equipment, used throughout all Regions of British Rail, is carried out. The section is also engaged on the design, development and production of equipment, using both ultrasonic and eddy current techniques.

In 1980 the Brighton maintenance depot had an allocation of 223 units, or 802 individual coaches. Target throughputs for monthly examinations were 46 units a week, and for three or four monthly, 12 units a week. The classes of units in the allocation were as follows:

Class (old designation in brackets)	No of units	Unit Nos
410 (4BEP)	10	7001-7010
414 (2HAP)	45	6019-6063
420 (4BIG)	19	7031-7049
421 (4CIG)	95	7301-36/58-64, 66-7406/27-38
423 (4VEP)	42	7721-31/81-87/ 7800-09/70-83
427 (4VEG)	12	7901-7912

Classes 410, 420, 421, 423 and 427 work main line services, combinations of 410, 420 and 421 forming the fast buffet car trains. Class 423 is widely employed on semi-fast and stopping services without buffets, although they can run in multiple with the other units if required. Class 427 is a version of Class 423 with increased luggage space gained by the removal of some seats and is primarily for Gatwick Airport portions. Class 414, a 2-car unit dating from 1956 (all the others are 4-car), is principally used on the Coastway services but can be coupled to any of the other classes based at Brighton to form a train of up to 12 coaches.

The depot also houses two 2-coach de-icing units, Nos 006 and 010, in which axle-driven pumps spray an oil-based fluid on the conductor to restrict the formation of ice, while scrapers remove any ice which may already have formed. When frosty conditions are predicted by the Meteorological Office the two units cover over 300 track-miles in a night along the Sussex coast and up to the Streatham/Wimbledon area.

Although Brighton had no locomotive allocation in 1980, it did have its 'own' locomotive, for on 3 December of that year Class 73/1 electro-diesel No 73.101 was named Brighton Evening Argus in a ceremony at Platform 7 in the station, so that Brighton joined the growing number of provincial centres with a locomotive named after their newspapers. The Argus had just celebrated its centenary, and as a link with this event the locomotive was temporarily renumbered 73.100 for the occasion. It worked to Willesden shortly afterwards – a movement duly reported to the TOPS computer, which suffered a minor convulsion on discovering that it already had the genuine 73.100 stored in its 'memory' at another location.

When colour-light signalling came to Brighton at the

Above left: **The Combined Engineering Depot on the site of the old steam shed between the west coast line (foreground) and the main line to London. The east coast line is on the extreme right.**

Above: **Class 73 No 73.100 *Brighton Evening Argus* at Brighton station prior to the naming ceremony, with the curtain fixture in position.** *Colin J. Marsden*

Centre right: **The locomotive nameplate.** *Colin J. Marsden*

Right: **Finale: The Lewes Road viaduct of the Kemp Town branch still stands in 1981, but stops abruptly.** *Author*

time of electrification the new signalbox was incorporated into an upper floor of the works buildings. With demolition of the works it was left perched on the old brickwork, which remained like the surviving walls of nearby Bramber Castle as no more than a token reminder of past glories. Such was the scene in the early 1980s, but work had already begun to concentrate control of 280 track-miles in the Central Division in a new power signalbox at Three Bridges. The area being resignalled adjoined the London Bridge and Victoria schemes, and on completion of the work in 1987 the boxes at Victoria and Three Bridges will control the whole route between Victoria and Brighton and adjacent sections – two boxes doing the work of 33. At the same time extensive rationalisation of track layouts is taking place. With these undertakings the operation of the Brighton line is being updated to meet the transport patterns of its time as effectively as it was with electrification 50 years ago.

Appendix 1
Allocations of Locomotives

1911. The pre-World War 1 service at its height

Class	Wheel arrangement	Numbers	Total
H1	4-4-2	37-41	5
H2	4-4-2	421-2	2
B4	4-4-0	45-7/50/3/60/5/71	8
B2	4-4-0	201/217	2
C	0-6-0	432/443	2
C2	0-6-0	440/3/9/52/524/33/9	7
A1	0-6-0T	159/60/65-8/635/8/42/3/4/7/74/7/8/681/2	17
E1	0-6-0T	98/9/109/18/9/20/3/33/5/41/8	11
B1	0-4-2	181/2/4/9/97-9/200/214/6/8-20	13
D2	0-4-2	300-3/5-8	8
D1	0-4-2T	223/8/53/7/67/81/614/25	8
J	4-6-2T	325	1
D3	0-4-4T	363/5/6/74/5/84/6/392/7	9
E3	0-6-2T	462	1
E4	0-6-2T	466/75/84/6/7/94/5/9/501/3/9/10/2/3/7	15
E5	0-6-2T	406	1
E6	0-6-2T	413	1
I1	4-4-2T	6	1
I1x	4-4-2T	95-99	5
I2	4-4-2T	13	1
I3	4-4-2T	25-7/30/75/7/80/1	8
I4	4-4-2T	35	1
		Total	127

1925. Early post-Grouping

Class	Wheel arrangement	Numbers	Total
H1	4-4-2	37-41	5
H2	4-4-2	421-26	5
B4	4-4-0	44/6/53/9/61/8	6
K	2-6-0	340/43/51/2	4
C2	0-6-0	526	1
C2x	0-6-0	441/4/9, 524/32/4/9/40/6	9
B1	0-4-2	174/6/81/4/7/93/7/618/9	9
D3	0-4-2	365/9/71/4/6/7/8/91	8
D3x	0-4-2	396/7	2
L	4-6-4T	327-33	7
'River'	2-6-4T	A790-4	5
J	4-6-2T	325/6	2
I1x	4-4-2T	596	1
I3	4-4-2T	21/7/8/78/82/3/9/91	8
E1	0-6-2T	116/29/36/8/9/44/7/52/609/86	10
E3	0-6-2T	158/69	2
E4	0-6-2T	475/80/1/5/95/9/501/7/9/10/16	11
A1x	0-6-0T	635/44/7	3

o Brighton mpd

D1	0-4-2T	258/77/80/362/617	5
D1m	0-4-2T	214/5/7/27/52/75/99/358/605/23/25/99	12
E1x	0-6-2T	689	1
		Total	124

May 1949. Second year of British Railways

Class	Wheel arrangement	Numbers	Total
8F (WD)	2-8-0	90247/307/54	4
WC	4-6-2	34037-40	4
K	2-6-0	32339/41-5	6
U1	2-6-0	31890-4/31900	6
H1	4-4-2	32039	1
H2	4-4-2	32421/2/4	3
C2x	0-6-0	32438/43/32523/28/39/43	6
I3	4-4-2T	32076/80/86/88	4
E1	0-6-2T	32127/39/606	3
E3	0-6-2T	32455	1
E4	0-6-2T	32470/1/86/91/32505/9/13/4/32566/7	10
E5	0-6-2T	32400/32576/7/83/87/91/4	7
D1	0-4-2T	32253	1
P	0-6-0T	31178/31325/31557	3
D3	0-4-4T	32368/72/6/86	4
		Total	63

November 1960

Class	Wheel arrangement	Numbers	Total
WC	4-6-2	34008/19/38	3
BoB	4-6-2	34055/7	2
K	2-6-0	32337-44	8
U1	2-6-0	31890/1	1
V	4-4-0	30901/7/11/17/19	5
A1	0-6-0T	32635/6	2
A1x	0-6-0T	32662/70	2
P	0-6-0T	31556	1
E4	0-6-2T	32468/75/9/32503/4/12/15/78/80	9
H	0-4-4T	31005/31276/31308/22/31530	5
M7	0-4-4T	30049-53/56/30110/328/379	9
C	0-6-0	31724	1
C2x	0-6-0	32441/9	2
BR4	2-6-4T	80013/31/2/3/43-54	16
O3	0-6-0	D2281/2/6	3
O8	0-6-0	D3093/4/D3217-21	7
		Total	76

m = mata fitted

143

Appendix 2
Brighton under Fire

Mr R. C. Riley, who was stationed at Brighton during World War 2, has kindly contributed the following reminiscences of air attacks on railway installations:

'I do not recall Brighton having any night raids but it was subject to daytime "hit and run" attacks. I watched a single fighter coming in off the sea from the roof of a seafront hotel and as it reared up, immediately above my head, certainly too close for comfort, I saw the black crosses on its wings! Then the firing began. The only time the shed suffered such an attack was on 12 October 1942. Class S15 4-6-0 No 836 was on the turntable at the time and got two or three cannon shells in the boiler side ahead of the firebox. It was hastily removed from the turntable and the fire thrown out. Four other engines suffered superficial damage from machine gun bullets, including the firepump engine No 2255, which was specially cared for by one of the women cleaners at the shed. These engines were patched up on shed, but No 836 went into the works, where it was repaired and returned to traffic within a fortnight.

'The worst raid was just before 12.30pm on 25 May 1943. Five bombs were dropped on railway property. One fell in the Upper Goods Yard, exploding among wagons; one on the incline road retaining wall south of the same yard; one in No 2 carriage siding, Lovers Walk; one on the London Road viaduct, destroying two brick arches at the London end; and one on the Pullman Car Company's works at Preston Park. As a result of this raid there was one fatality among company staff; 43 electric coaches were damaged at Lovers Walk; five Pullman cars were badly damaged, three of which were later broken up, while 12 others sustained some degree of damage. Some 40 wagons were damaged in the goods yard, two beyond repair. Owing to burnt cables, current was off between Brighton and Preston Park, also between Preston Park and Hove, but this was restored four hours later. Two 2BIL sets and a PAN set were derailed at Lovers Walk, where four sidings were blocked, as also the main running lines, although these were cleared within six hours. A press report released some time later said that 30 fighter-bombers were involved in the raid.' [Other reports give the number actually engaged at Brighton as six.]

Mr Riley recalls walking over the viaduct in July, when from the sleepers one could still see down into the street below. It was a slightly hair-raising experience, but any misgivings about the track carrying the 'U1' 2-6-0 which headed the train on which he travelled the same evening fortunately proved unfounded. He was informed that when traffic was restored after the raid the temporary repair was tested by two LBSC Atlantics. Complete rebuilding of the damaged arches took four months and during that time a 15mph speed restriction was in force.